THE AIR FORCE ROLE IN

LOW-INTENSITY CONFLICT

by

DAVID J. DEAN
Lieutenant Colonel, USAF
Airpower Research Institute

Air University
Air University Press
Maxwell Air Force Base, Alabama 36112-5532

October 1986

Library of Congress Cataloging in Publication Data

Dean, David J.
   The Air Force Role in Low-Intensity Conflict.

   At head of title: Center for Aerospace Doctrine, Research, and Education.
   "October 1986."
   Includes bibliographies and index.
   1. Air warfare. 2. Low-intensity conflicts. 3. Aeronautics, Military—Morocco—History. 4. Morocco—History—20th century. 5. Military assistance, American—Morocco. I. Air University (U.S.). Center for Aerospace Doctrine, Research, and Education. II. Title.
   UG630.D38   1986   358.4'14   86-17498

ISBN 1-58566-014-0

> First Printing October 1986
> Second Printing April 1992
> Third Printing March 1999
> Fourth Printing June 2001

DISCLAIMER

This study represents the views of the author and does not necessarily reflect the official opinion of the Air University Center for Aerospace Doctrine, Research, and Education (CADRE) or the Department of the Air Force. This publication has been reviewed by security and policy review authorities and is cleared for public release.

For sale by the Superintendent of Documents
US Government Printing Office
Washington DC 20402

CONTENTS

Chapter		Page
	DISCLAIMER	ii
	FOREWORD	ix
	ABOUT THE AUTHOR	xi
	PREFACE	xiii
	ACKNOWLEDGMENTS	xv
1	LOW-INTENSITY CONFLICT: WHAT IS IT AND WHY SHOULD IT CONCERN THE USAF?	1
	Low-Intensity Conflict Defined	1
	Special Characteristics of Low-Intensity Conflict	7
	Operational Terms Relating to Low-Intensity Conflict	8
	Future Conflicts	11
	Dealing with Future Conflict	13
	Notes	17
2	AIR POWER IN SMALL WARS: THE BRITISH AIR CONTROL EXPERIENCE	19
	Air Control's Genesis	19
	Air Control: From Concept to Doctrine	22
	The Requirements of British Air Control	24
	Air Control and Today's US Air Force	25
	Notes	27

Chapter		Page
3	THE MOROCCO-POLISARIO WAR: A CASE STUDY OF A MODERN LOW-INTENSITY CONFLICT	29
	Resources and Topography of Western Sahara	29
	Moroccan Claims and Stakes in Western Sahara	31
	The Polisario Front	34
	Algeria	35
	Mauritania	36
	Libya	37
	France	38
	The United States	38
	Peripheral Players	39
	The War's Importance	40
	Evolution of the War	41
	Notes	53
4	THE ROYAL MOROCCAN AIR FORCE AND UNITED STATES' ASSISTANCE	55
	The Royal Moroccan Air Force in Moroccan Politics	55
	Building Up the Royal Moroccan Air Force	57
	The Force	59
	Limitations of the RMAF	62
	United States Assistance to the Royal Moroccan Air Force ..	65
	Meeting the SA-6 Threat	67
	Notes	71
5	MILITARY REQUIREMENTS FOR LOW-INTENSITY CONFLICTS: LESSONS FROM MOROCCO	73
	Imprecise US Policies and Objectives	74
	Basic Requirements for Assisting a Third World Air Force ..	76
	Levels of Potential Air Force Participation	78
	Notes	83

Chapter		Page
6	EARLY LOW-INTENSITY CONFLICT EFFORTS BY THE USAF: THE SPECIAL AIR WARFARE CENTER	85
	Foundation of Air Force Role in Low-Intensity Conflict......	85
	In Search of an Air Force Role in Small Wars	87
	Creation of Jungle Jim	88
	The Special Air Warfare Center: Its Origin, Expansion, and Growth	89
	A Time of Organizational Change	94
	Vietnam Devours Special Air Warfare Center Assets	98
	Lessons from the Special Air Warfare Center	99
	Notes	103
7	A PLAN FOR USAF PARTICIPATION IN LOW-INTENSITY CONFLICT	105
	Committing the Organization	106
	Doctrine and Philosophy	110
	A Special Air Warfare Center for Today's World.............	112
	Looking Ahead	119
	Notes	127

LIST OF ILLUSTRATIONS

Figure		Page
1	Sarkesian's Conflict Spectrum	3
2	US Army Definition of Low-Intensity Conflict	5
3	Conflict Spectrum Defined in Terms of US Military Operations	6
4	North Africa	32
5	F-15—US Supplied Fighter of the Royal Moroccan Air Force	43
6	A Portion of the Ceinture Near Bu-Craâ	48
7	A Portion of the Ceinture Near Bu-Craâ	48
8	Close-ups of Defensive Positions Along Ceinture	49
9	Close-ups of Defensive Positions Along Ceinture	49
10	Reference Map: Saharan War	50
11	Pilot Production in 1982	60
12	Pilot Production in 1982	61
13	Organizational Chart—Special Air Warfare Center	90
14	Infrastructure	113

Figure *Page*

15	Operations	118
16	A-37 Low-Level Attack Fighter	120
17	C-7A Caribou Short Takeoff and Landing Transport	121
18	C-128 Provider Attack Transport	122
19	OV-10 Light-Armed Reconnaissance and Attack Aircraft	123
20	Hierarchy of War Fighting	125

FOREWORD

In the last few decades, the third world countries of Africa, Asia, the Middle East, and the Pacific Basin have become increasingly important in world affairs. Because the third world is a major source of many natural resources vital to the industries of the United States and its allies and because many third world countries occupy critical geostrategic points around the globe, it is the object of intense competition for political, economic, and military influence between the West and the Soviet bloc. This struggle for influence accompanies widespread economic depression and seemingly perpetual political instability, conditions which make the third world a ripe target for conflict—internal revolution, proxy wars between East and West, or even direct intervention by or conflict between the superpowers.

These conflicts have taken the form of guerrilla wars (national wars of revolution or even counterrevolution), direct intervention (Grenada, the Dominican Republic, Afganistan, Chad, and Vietnam), and military assistance and advisory activities (El Salvador, Angola, Nicaragua, and Morocco). In recent years military and political thinkers have seen these examples of political-military conflict as presenting a new category of conflict that is not adequately addressed in current US military doctrine, strategy, and planning. Because of the high probability of involvement in third world conflicts in the near future, the US military must devote a much larger share of its resources to adapting its organization, doctrine, strategy, and planning to meet the flexibility and innovation that low-intensity conflict missions will demand.

Colonel Dean's study makes a significant contribution to the growing body of literature on low-intensity conflict. He offers many insights to the challenges that low-intensity conflict presents to the Air Force. His proposal to reestablish the Special Air Warfare Center deserves serious thought and study.

DONALD D. STEVENS
Colonel, USAF
Commander
Center for Aerospace Doctrine,
   Research, and Education

ABOUT THE AUTHOR

Lt Col David J. Dean is an action officer in the Plans and Policy Directorate, Organization of the Joint Chiefs of Staff. A graduate of the Georgetown University School of Foreign Service (BSFS) and Florida State University (MA), Lieutenant Colonel Dean has served in maintenance, intelligence, and international politico-military affairs assignments during his Air Force career.

PREFACE

This book grew from an opportunity to study a third world air force fighting an externally supported insurgency. The players were the Royal Moroccan Air Force and the Polisario, the latter trying to wrest control of the Western Sahara from the Kingdom of Morocco. The United States has also been a player in the Morocco-Polisario war as the source of much of Morocco's war material, especially the weapons used by the Royal Moroccan Air Force. Help from the United States was especially important when the Polisario deployed Soviet-built SA-6 surface-to-air missiles to counter the growing effectiveness of the Royal Moroccan Air Force. For many reasons, the United States and the US Air Force were not able to assist the Moroccans effectively.

The Morocco-Polisario-US scenario that provides the basis for this study was a tiny aspect of US foreign and military policy in the early 1980s. But it shows a political-military problem that deserves a good deal of thought now. That problem simply stated is: How is the United States going to exert political-military influence in the third world during the next twenty years? Clearly, overall US influence in the third world will be a combination of political, military, economic, and social activity. But the military, in many cases, will be the most visible form of assistance, and one upon which the recipient nation will depend for immediate results. Are the military components as instruments of national policy able to act effectively in the third world? If not, what needs to be done?

The US Air Force (and the other services) needs to consider the question of effective assistance to third world countries as part of a basic shift in strategic thinking. Our primary strategic planning effort has been to insert large numbers of US ground and air forces into an area such as the Persian Gulf to accomplish our policy objectives. That planning effort must continue, but with the understanding that inserting a major US force in any third world region is extremely unlikely, both for domestic political reasons and because potential host nations are reluctant to support large US forces. Our primary strategic focus for planning needs to shift to providing effective leverage for third world friends and allies. That leverage can be in the form of arms sales, training, doctrine, or even small specialized forces. But providing leverage depends on effective planning that builds the data base which allows us to pinpoint the host country's needs and capabilities. Developing that kind of expertise in the USAF, and in the other services, will be a difficult and frustrating long-term proposition. The Air Force must recognize the need for a change and must act upon it. Planning to exert effective political-military influence in the third world may not be a glamorous task, but it will be the name of the game for the next twenty years and beyond. This book offers some ideas in that regard.

DAVID J. DEAN
Lt Col, USAF

ACKNOWLEDGMENTS

Col Ken Alnwick, USAF, is the godfather of this book. It was he who led the Air University expedition to Morocco to study the role of the Royal Moroccan Air Force in the Morocco—Polisario conflict and who picked me to be the "Morocco expert" for the trip. Colonel Alnwick also introduced me to the mysteries of small wars and low-intensity conflict. Those who have helped me understand the difficulties of military organizations coping with unfamiliar ways of war are too numerous to mention. But the first to push me into questioning conventional wisdom and traditional approaches to analyzing problems deserves my special thanks—the late Professor Carroll Quigley of Georgetown University. Finally, Mr Tom Lobenstein of the Air University Center for Aerospace Doctrine, Research, and Education, an editor *par excellence,* deserves great credit for his manful struggle to make this book coherent.

CHAPTER 1

LOW-INTENSITY CONFLICT: WHAT IS IT AND WHY SHOULD IT CONCERN THE USAF?

I believe that the low intensity conflict is the most important strategic issue facing the US. If we don't learn to deal with it, we risk being isolated in an increasingly competitive world. . . .[1]

General Wallace H. Nutting, USA

What is low-intensity conflict? Why is General Nutting so concerned about it? Is it counterinsurgent warfare, that form of conflict which the United States failed to master and win in Southeast Asia? Is low-intensity conflict something we should avoid lest the Vietnam-related social, political, and military upheavals of the 1960s and 1970s be relived in the 1980s and 1990s? Or in the years ahead, will the world be such that the United States must prepare for a form of conflict that is not pristinely dualistic—good confronting evil, with clear-cut, "vital" national interests or national survival at stake? To answer these questions we must begin by attempting to understand the concept of low-intensity conflict and the kinds of military, paramilitary, political, and economic activity it encompasses.

Low-Intensity Conflict Defined

Professor Sam Sarkesian of the Loyola University of Chicago has done more than anyone to try to establish a meaningful definition of low-intensity conflict. Getting agreement on what exactly is meant by low-intensity conflict proved to be the toughest issue faced by participants at a 1979 workshop at Loyola. The best they could do was to adopt a working definition.

> Low-intensity conflict . . . refers to the range of activities and operations on the lower end of the conflict spectrum involving the use of military or a variety of semi-military forces (both combat and noncombat) on the part of the intervening power to influence and compel the adversary to accept a political-military condition.[2]

This definition presupposes an area within a conflict spectrum and an intervening power seeking to impose its will in a given situation. Sarkesian depicts a spectrum of conflict (fig. 1) ranging between noncombatant force employment and today's ultimate form of conflict, strategic nuclear war.[3] Sarkesian is not clear as to when a low-intensity conflict graduates to a mid- or high-intensity one. Presumably a break point between wars of lower and higher intensity would occur in a Vietnam-type conflict when the intervening power made the decision to commit division-sized ground force units and wing-sized air force units. At such a point, a conflict would no longer be defined as low-intensity because major national resources are being committed to the conflict.

Sarkesian's conflict spectrum identifies three levels of US participation in guerrilla warfare. During the first phase, Guerrilla I, US forces would be involved in a purely advisory role; military advisory teams would work with a host country to establish a useful level of proficiency in handling weapons applicable to the type of conflict being experienced. At this level of conflict the United States might also provide training in tactics and doctrine. When US forces begin serving as cadre or "stiffeners" for local forces, then the level of conflict would clearly move into the Guerrilla II level of involvement. At this stage, special operations forces from any or all US services could work with specific host country units as they developed and executed operations in the field. The highest stage of US involvement in guerrilla war, Guerrilla III, would see integration of complete US combat units with indigenous forces. Presumably, this level of activity would be the highest in which the United States could become involved without a declaration of war. Thus, Sarkesian defines low-intensity conflict as a range along the conflict spectrum where a variety of military and paramilitary activities take place to achieve limited political goals—usually to assist a threatened friend.

In contrast, the US Army defines low-intensity conflict differently and in terms that emphasize operational rather than theoretical uses of force. The Army recognizes two levels of low-intensity conflict: Type A and Type B. Type A requires *assistance operations by US combat forces* to "establish, regain, or maintain control of specific land areas threatened by guerrilla warfare, revolution, subversion, or other tactics aimed at internal seizure of power." Type B conflicts require *"US advice, combat support,* and *combat service support* for indigenous or allied forces facing the same kind of threat described in Type A conflicts." In the Army's definition of mid- and high-intensity conflicts, a state of war between nations would exist. The difference between mid- and high-intensity conflicts is the nature of the objectives involved, the level of force that may be applied, and the size of the geographic area that might be involved.

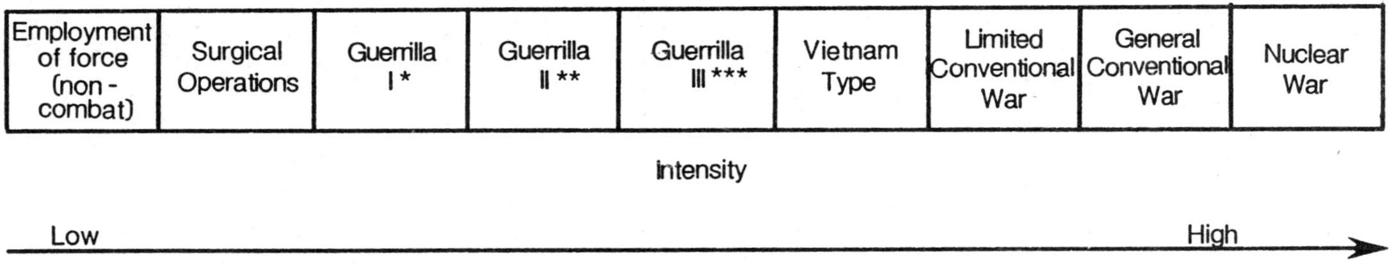

LOW-INTENSITY CONFLICT

| Employment of force (non-combat) | Surgical Operations | Guerrilla I* | Guerrilla II** | Guerrilla III*** | Vietnam Type | Limited Conventional War | General Conventional War | Nuclear War |

Low ←——— Intensity ———→ High

Guerrilla I: Weapons Assistance Teams - Police Training - Advisory Teams

Guerrilla II: Special Forces Teams - Cadre for Indigenous Forces (Continuation of Guerrilla I)

Guerrilla III: Integration of US Combat Units with Indigenous Forces (Continuation of Guerrilla I and II).

All Guerrilla classifications include requisite economic assistance.

Figure 1. Sarkesian's Conflict Spectrum.

The Army considers a worst case insurgency situation such as Vietnam as one where a higher classification than low-intensity conflict may apply.[4] Figure 2 illustrates the Army's definition of the various levels of conflict.

Both Sarkesian's and the Army's definitions of low-intensity conflict are useful. Sarkesian looks at the issue from the standpoint of a US decision maker who needs to make policy decisions on what is to be done to help a threatened friend. The Army's approach is a more prosaic one that makes a fundamental distinction between two responses to low-intensity conflict: Will Army forces be assigned to help a country by fighting or by advising? The Army thus limits low-intensity conflict to involvement of the United States in a country requiring assistance; the Army's definition does not include the related ideas of US participation in peacekeeping duties, shows of force, or unilateral US intervention in a second country.

For the purposes of this paper, a fairly broad range of activity will be considered as low-intensity conflict. Our definition will lean more to Sarkesian than to the Army. Figure 3 shows the kinds of activities US forces may be asked to accomplish in low-intensity conflict situations. As the chart suggests, the Unites States should have forces designed to show resolve without engaging in combat, to accomplish specialized operations such as the Son Tay raid, and to assist friendly countries facing threats to their internal security by providing advisory assistance, cadre, and, ultimately, US combat units that can be integrated with those of the host nation. In addition, the United States should have the ability to intervene unilaterally in other countries as the need arises. Such intervention will be most likely in the third world. The primary purpose in any such intervention would be to impose American will on a third world situation. Although the notion of US intervention abroad, either unilaterally or in concert with other forces, is not particularly popular in this country at this time, and it is a capability our military needs to perfect, as proven in Grenada.

Counterterrorism is included in figure 3, although it is not included in the definition of low-intensity conflict. Historically, terrorism has most often been the approach taken by individuals or groups seeking to make a random political statement or to commit an act of violence to support a vision of future revolutionary change. Most often police forces rather than the military are in charge of counterterrorist operations. However, terrorism could be part of an insurgent group's repertoire of tactics and thus could be part of the problem faced by US assistance forces—but not the primary problem for which the forces were sent.

The more dangerous form of terrorism currently evolving in the Middle East is state-sponsored terrorism, or terrorism that is an integral part of a strategy which has both clear political objectives and the backing of sovereign states. Hence, US forces that confront it will require special training and capabilities. As a result of the bombing of the Marine barracks at the Beirut International Airport on 23 October 1983, this country is devoting considerable attention to the

LOW-INTENSITY CONFLICT

LOW-INTENSITY B	LOW-INTENSITY A	SOUTHEAST ASIA TYPE	MID-INTENSITY	HIGH-INTENSITY
US advice, combat support, combat service support for host nations.	US combat forces supporting host nation threatened by guerilla warfare, revolution, subversion.	Insurgency involving several nations, out-side forces.	War between nations with limited objectives, limited force.	Unlimited war between nations.
LOWEST				HIGHEST

Figure 2. US Army Definition of Low-Intensity Conflict.

THE AIR FORCE ROLE IN LOW-INTENSITY CONFLICT

	Noncombat Force Employment	One-Time Operations	Advisory Assistance	Cadre for Host Forces	Combat Units with Host Forces	Unilateral Intervention	Limited Conventional War	Unlimited Conventional War	Nuclear War
	-Joint exercise -Show of force -Increased alert -Peace keeping -Combat support -Intelligence -Logistics -Foreign military sales	-Son Tay-type raids	-Short term military training teams -No combat -Expedited foreign military sales	-Longer term teams in field	-Battalion/ squadron size units -Special Operations Force units	-Carrier battle group -Specialized joint units -Short term specific goal established	-Full Rapid Deployment Joint Task Force employment		

COUNTER-TERRORISM ⟵⎯⎯⎯⎯⎯ LOW INTENSITY ⎯⎯⎯⎯⎯ MID INTENSITY ⎯⎯⎯⎯⎯ HIGH INTENSITY

Figure 3. Conflict Spectrum Defined in Terms of US Military Operations.

problems of counterterrorism. Nevertheless, this paper concentrates on a wider concept—low-intensity conflict—and the special problems it presents, since that form of conflict involves such a great range of challenges for the military, as opposed to the very difficult but more focused challenges of counterterrorism.

Special Characteristics of Low-Intensity Conflict

Several characteristics of conflict make them "low-intensity" from the US point of view. The issues that will be involved such a conflict will probably not be "vital" US interests. Vital security interests can be defined in many ways. The fundamental distinction between vital and other interests is that a nation will go to war over the former but not the latter. In a low-intensity conflict, it is conceivable that a vital interest could be at stake—perhaps access to oil or some specific mineral. However, it would be much more likely that a low-intensity conflict would not center on a vital interest, at least insofar as US involvement was concerned. And although the US government might claim that a vital interest is at stake, it would have difficulty convincing the American public and its representatives in Congress that such a condition existed, thus making a declaration of war by the United States impossible. For instance, recent activity in El Salvador and the US involvement there clearly falls into the realm of low-intensity conflict. The United States government is trying to sell an increased level of involvement to the nation on the basis that we are protecting a vital US interest—keeping all of Latin America from succumbing to Soviet-inspired revolutionary movements. US public opinion has a difficult time believing that what is happening in El Salvador has any direct relevance to this country. It may become necessary and even prudent to defend the notion that US military involvement in small wars may be justified even if a vital US interest is not at stake. The international perception that the United States can and will act militarily in a whole range of ways, from assisting friends to actual intervention to defend an important but not vital interest, is one this country may want to foster in the years ahead.

Besides normally involving nonvital US interests, other characteristics of low-intensity conflict distinguish it from the more familiar limited and strategic conflicts that consume so much of the military's attention and energy. A low-intensity conflict would likely be limited in geographic area, have few participants, and be of limited duration; any US military operations contemplated would be accomplished by small, specialized units. The most common type of low-intensity conflict would be a war of insurgency or a limited conventional conflict on a scale smaller than Vietnam. US forces would likely be assisting friendly countries rather than managing the conflict unilaterally. Should a small war escalate to a level where larger US formations were involved (above battalion or squadron size), the objectives and management of the conflict would shift the level to the intervention level (fig. 3) and an expanded US effort to control the war rather than merely assisting a friend would be expected.

By discussing low-intensity conflict in terms of operational responses and limiting parameters (time, level of resources involved, geography, and related variables), we have a foundation for a working definition of the term. That is, low-intensity conflict is a wide range of political-military activity that aims to accomplish limited political and military objectives without resorting to a declaration of war or committing large-scale US forces (or nuclear weapons) to the fray. The United States can participate in such conflicts in several ways: using military forces in noncombat operations to show support, resolve, or intent; advising and assisting a host government; and intervening with specialized combat forces. Thus in low-intensity conflicts US policymakers can use military forces to accomplish political objectives without using massive resources, and can do so at a controllable level of escalation. Most US military responses to low-intensity conflict would be drawn from Department of Defense special operations forces. Only when the stage of unilateral intervention had been reached would general purpose forces be employed—and then the primary forces (at this time) would be marine and naval air resources. The Strategic Air Command's strategic projection force might come into play as well.

Operational Terms Relating to Low-Intensity Conflict

Two terms, special operations and special air warfare, are often used to describe low-intensity warfare operations in the US Air Force. Both are umbrella terms, as is low-intensity conflict itself. Special operations is defined in the 1979 version of Joint Chiefs of Staff Publication 1 (JCS Pub 1) simply as "secondary or supporting operations which may be adjuncts to various other operations and for which no one service is assigned primary responsibility."[5] A recent draft of JCS Pub 20, volume 1, includes a new definition:

> Special Operations (SO) is defined as operations conducted by specially trained, equipped, and organized Department of Defense forces against strategic or tactical targets in pursuit of national military, political, economic, or psychological objectives. These operations may be conducted during periods of peace or hostilities. They may support conventional military operations, or they may be prosecuted independently when the use of conventional forces is either inappropriate or infeasible. Special operations may include unconventional warfare (UW), counterterrorist operations, collective security (foreign internal defense [FID]), psychological operations, direct action missions, and intelligent (strategic and tactical) reporting.[6]

Clearly, special operations are given a much wider area of operations under the new definition. Especially noteworthy is the idea that special operations may be independent of conventional operations and may include civil affairs measures as well as collective security, a new term in the context of special operations. Special operations apparently has replaced special air warfare, the latter being an Air Force term referring to the air aspects of counterinsurgency, unconventional warfare, and psychological operations. This change has two effects: it gives all the US military services the same generic term for special operations and it erodes the idea that air power can play an independent or unique role in special operations. Moreover, this shift in terminology seems to signify an Air Force realization that special air warfare was an outmoded concept. (It was last defined in Air Force Manual [AFM] 2–5, *Tactical Air Operations/Special Air Warfare* [1967], and does not appear in any more recent manuals.)

Several specific types special operations of military have been subsumed under the umbrella of special operations, and formerly under special air warfare. For example, unconventional warfare is occasionally used interchangeably with low-intensity conflict or special operations. It should not be. Unconventional warfare traditionally concerns activities conducted within enemy-held or -controlled territory.[7] Its major element is guerrilla warfare, which involves military and paramilitary operations conducted in enemy-held territory by irregular, predominantly indigenous, forces. Escape and evasion, sabotage, and other low-visibility operations comprise the other main aspects of unconventional warfare.[8]

For another example, counterguerrilla activity in the past has been associated with the term counterinsurgency, more familiarly known by the acronym COIN. But because of negative connotations from Vietnam, counterinsurgency has become a nonword in the lexicon of special operations forces. This development represents a significant change, since in the the 1960s counterinsurgency was a discipline separate from unconventional warfare and included all "military, paramilitary, political, economic, psychological, and civic actions taken by a government to defeat subversive insurgency."[9] Today, by contrast, counterinsurgency does not appear in the Army manual, *Low-Intensity Conflict* (FM 100–20), or in the Air Force's Tactical Air Command Manual (TACM) 2–1, *Tactical Air Operations*, which presents the current doctrine for US Air Force special operations forces. Moreover, the Army's new definitions of low-intensity conflict, cited earlier, cover counterinsurgency (without using the term) by describing low-intensity conflict as operations to "establish, regain, or maintain control of areas threatened by guerrilla warfare, revolution, subversion, or other tactics aimed at internal seizure of power."[10] Thus, an important distinction between counterinsurgency and unconventional warfare is the area of operations for each: in the former, forces are supporting the incumbent government and are operating in territory they at least nominally hold, while in the latter they operate to overthrow the incumbent government in enemy-held territory.

An important aspect of counterinsurgency and other forms of low-intensity conflict has been the ability of the United States to provide a threatened country with appropriate arms, training, and advice. Then, in theory, the threatened country could handle the threat without US combat forces. Collective security is now being used to describe that kind of assistance effort.

The term collective security in the latest JCS definition of special operations seems to be an acceptable substitute for the Vietnam-era term foreign internal defense (FID). The 1979 version of JCS Pub 1 defined foreign internal defense as "participation by civilian and military agencies of a government in any of the action programs taken by another government to free and protect its society from subversion, lawlessness, and insurgency."[11] The Army continues to adhere to this definition in its own statements of doctrine and strategy.[12] The Air Force, however, defines foreign internal defense as "operations conducted on request from a foreign government . . . to aid allied nations . . . attain an established level of military self-reliance. FID is an extension of the Security Assistance Program, which is often tied to foreign military sales or grant-in-aid programs."[13] The Army and JCS definitions encompass more than the Air Force one and suggest nation-building programs by a wide variety of agencies. The Air Force definition is more narrow and suggests an "air force building" mission in a client country. It also tends to push this mission on to the security assistance program, a Defense Department program that makes it difficult to pinpoint foreign internal defense responsibility and expertise within the Air Force. Assumed in both definitions, however, is the notion that US agencies and armed services must be able to effectively transfer techniques, knowledge, and concepts to the armed forces of other countries to improve their internal and external capabilities.

The final term that invariably crops up when discussing special operations is psychological operations. Most writing on low-intensity conflict includes psychological operations as a discrete discipline, separate from counterinsurgency or unconventional warfare or foreign internal defense. Psychological operations are designed to influence friendly governments and people to support US national objectives or to have a negative effect on the enemy. Such actions can be passive or active and are designed to affect the emotions, attitudes, and behavior of the target population.[14] Thus, psychological operations should be considered part of *every* operation conducted along the low-intensity conflict spectrum. Psychological warfare should not be considered as a step along an escalatory process going from, for instance, a show of force to military advisors to intervention. Rather, it is a capability and a resource that must be exploited in any military operation. Therefore, it is not included as a separate entity in figure 3, which shows the kinds of potential US operations involved in low-intensity conflicts.

Future Conflicts

Thus, as the above discussion shows, low-intensity conflict remains a somewhat nebulous concept. Since it may encompass a vast range of military functions, we must ask: What are the most likely kinds of conflict the United States will be involved in over the next 20 years or so?

It seems inescapable that conflict at the lower end of the conflict spectrum is the most likely form of warfare over the next 20 years. *Air Force 2000*, one of the many documents projecting the future of conflict, notes that low-level conflict, which spans the political military spectrum from nonviolent political unrest to intense civil war, will frequently threaten US interests. The potential for low-level conflict will increase.[15] The reasons that make low-intensity conflict, or small wars, the most likely form of conflict in the years ahead are many.

The current and projected military balance between the United States and the USSR and between NATO and the Warsaw Pact makes small wars more likely than large ones. The strategic nuclear balance between the superpowers has reached a balance-of-terror level. Both sides have enormous holdings of nuclear warheads that can be delivered in many ways. Neither side truly comprehends the effects of a large-scale nuclear strike in terms of achievable military goals. Thus, the probability of successfully using nuclear arsenals to achieve policy goals is uncertain enough to make their use unlikely. However, maintaining a balance in comparative nuclear strength is necessary to ensure that neither side could reduce this uncertainty to a level where initiating a nuclear attack could become a realistic policy option.

To a lesser extent, the same sort of standoff exists in the Western European and Korean theaters. These theaters could be flashpoints for a major nonnuclear (or at least initially nonnuclear) war. Massive conventional forces, backed up by the threat of nuclear escalation, face each other in the NATO-Warsaw Pact area. This standoff has held for more than 30 years. The Soviets are facing powerful centrifugal forces in their European empire that will occupy a good deal of their resources and attention in the years ahead. Although these forces may encourage increased Soviet repression in their empire that could increase tension between Moscow and NATO, the balance of forces between the two alliances is such that neither side could be assured of a quick or easy victory. Certainly the balance of forces in Europe and the need to maintain credible deterrent forces to keep the Warsaw Pact at bay in central Europe is a prime policy concern for the United States. In recent years, the US military has expended vast resources in improving NATO's war-fighting capability, and justifiably so since American and European security, well-being, and cultural values are so closely interwined.

But, even though maintaining the standoff in Europe must be at the top of US security concerns, the likelihood of a war erupting there is low.[16]

The standoff in Korea, the other potential flashpoint where large US forces are committed on site, is more fragile than the one in Europe but nonetheless quite stable. South Korea's economy continues to grow rapidly while the North's economy, strangled by defense commitments, continues to stagnate.[17] The current military balance favors the North, but the South is making enormous strides in weapon production capabilities and adopting advanced technologies into its forces. These factors plus the continued presence of US ground, air, and naval forces suggests that stability rather than war is the likely course of events on that troubled peninsula for the next decade or two. The fly in the ointment of that projection is the impossibility of forecasting the intentions of North Korea's leader Kim Il-Sung.

Kim could well believe that because of his increasing age and the growing relative strength of Seoul vis-à-vis Pyŏngyang he should make one last attempt to unite the peninsula under his control. Possible political instability in Seoul, brought on by the repressive tendencies of the current South Korean regime, may provide an opportunity for Kim, although he was either unwilling or unable to exploit such a situation when President Park Chung Hee was assassinated in December 1979. However, even assuming a strong North Korean desire to unite the Koreans by force, the deterrence posed by the formidable South Korean military, backed up by considerable US force, should make conflict in Korea only slightly more likely than a NATO-Warsaw Pact war for the next 20 years.

The standoff situation that exists in Europe and Korea seems unlikely to change significantly in the years ahead. US and allied forces have spent vast resources on materials, strategic planning, and tactical readiness to ensure that the standoff endures. The interests of both the United States and the USSR are well served if conflicts that could threaten either country's vital national interests, which theoretically could lead to a nuclear exchange, are avoided.

This being so, the area where the United States and USSR will likely be competing in the future will be among the lesser-developed countries of the third world, especially in Latin America, Africa, and the Middle East. The third world will be an area of contention for the superpowers for many reasons. Economic factors, however, tend to dominate any discussion as to why the third world is and will be important to the United States. With the growing interdependence of the world economies, greater volumes of raw materials and finished goods move among nations than ever before.[18] The stability of that flow strongly influences US production programs, standards of living, and prices. Because disruptions can have a direct impact on American and allied economies, the need to apply force to maintain the flow may be required.

A related fact is that heavy industries are moving outside the industrialized democracies. The United States and Western Europe may well be on their way into a postindustrial revolution that will see increasing emphasis on high-technology products and less on such traditional heavy industry as steel production. In the last decade, more than 90 percent of new basic industrial capacity such as steel and aluminum plants has been built outside the United States.[19] Access to these new plants could eventually become as important to the United States as was Japanese access to American scrap steel in 1940. The United States may have to apply force to guarantee access to the materials American industry needs and to ensure access to oil and strategic minerals as well. Military force will certainly be part of any program designed to assure access to resources abroad.

Economic issues and potential conflicts over access to resources and industrial capacity must be considered in terms of the political realities in the third world. The demands of population growth, rising expectations fueled by the explosion in mass communications, and the difficulty of satisfying basic human needs is already stretching the resources of many third world countries. Political instability in many of these countries will be likely as governments fail to meet the demands of their people; this instability could range between uncontrolled migrations resulting from famines and violent internal attempts to change governments. The Soviet Union and its proxies will likely be involved either as instigators or supporters of revolutionary movements or, in the case of Soviet proxies, as actual participants in such movements.

The weapons available to even small revolutionary groups, to third world military organizations in general, and to Soviet proxy forces will make participation by US forces or US client states especially difficult. Sophisticated arms have been flowing to the third world from the United States, USSR, and other arms producers for years. Even though most third world countries have not developed the techniques and infrastructure to fully use the weapons they have obtained, the mere presence in third world forces of quality aircraft, tanks, artillery, and surface-to-air missiles (SAMs) makes the potential destructive capability very great. Highly capable SAMs are now available to even the smallest insurgent organization and can be used to great effect in third world conflicts.

Thus, it seems that a combination of factors will make low-intensity conflict a very likely phenomenon in the years ahead. Preparing for a wide range of conflict in the third world would be a prudent plan for the United States.

Dealing with Future Conflict

In a speech to the 1983 Air Force Long-Range Planning Conference, Congressman Newt Gingrich, a distinguished scholar as well as a legislator, spoke of four hierarchical layers of decision making and planning relating to conflict.[20] At the top of the hierarchy is vision, followed by strategy, operations, and tactics. He suggested that military art is related to vision and strategy while operations and tactics are oriented to military science. He further suggested that achieving effective vision and strategy is more difficult and more important than having good operations and tactics. Representative Gingrich used the example of Vietnam to illustrate his concept. In his view, the North Vietnamese won at the vision and strategy level; we won at the operational and tactical level. The congressman suggested that we need to focus on small wars at all four levels of this hierarchy if we are to survive in the years ahead.

Yet little is written about the "vision" and the "strategy" of the United States for the future in any context, and especially so in the context of low-intensity conflict or small wars. At the most prosaic level, a vision that makes some sense for the United States in the context of low-intensity conflict is to assume that as a nation we may need to be able to impose our will selectively in the third world during the next 20 years and beyond. The volatility of the newly developing countries will be such that disruptions to lines of supply coupled with the vulnerability of key areas to Soviet or Soviet-proxy influence will require a US response. The only hint we in the military have that such a vision for small wars exists is the fact that high-level directives such as the *Defense Guidance* require the military to prepare to fight all across the conflict spectrum.

Vision must come from the highest leadership level in the government. For example, it was John F. Kennedy who stated so clearly that the United States was going to fight communist insurgencies—wars of national liberation—whenever required. He pressured the US military to develop forces that the counterinsurgency mission, both to assist beleaguered friends and to use in direct action where required. That early counterinsurgency effort foundered in Vietnam. Of the many difficulties with our participating in the Vietnam conflict, however, the lack of a national vision on what we hoped to accomplish there seems fundamental. Without a clear vision of what we hoped to accomplish, a strategy—an overall plan for bringing all the elements of national power to bear to achieve an objective—could not be developed.

The United States is in such a position today in regard to low-intensity conflict. The scars of Vietnam are still severe. Because of the Vietnam syndrome, most talk of assisting a third world country or intervening in the third world will likely be met with the response that we can never allow a tragedy like Vietnam to occur again.[21] Yet, at the same time, Americans are beginning to realize the importance of the third world to the economic well-being of the United States and the need to maintain stability in such areas as Latin America, Africa, and the Middle East. The years following Vietnam saw the US military concentrate on building forces neglected during the Vietnam conflict. The emphasis on spending and planning went almost exclusively to modernizing strategic nuclear forces and rebuilding, reequipping, and training forces designed for the anticipated high-intensity, incredibly crowded and complex battlefield of Central Europe. That effort could be justified to the American people in terms of "vital interests" without grating too harshly on their noninterventionist sensibilities, which were still smarting from Vietnam.

If Frank Klingberg, a leading authority on alternating moods in US foreign policy is correct, by the end of the 1980s the United States will have passed from an "introvert" or noninterventionist phase back into an "extrovert" phase. The extrovert phase will be marked by a general realization that the United States must be able to exercise US military power abroad.[22] Klingberg assumes that over the intervening years, a "vision" will develop in the United States which will include a demand that this country should be able to enforce its will in the third world via diplomatic, economic, and, if necessary, military means. We in the military cannot generate such a vision among the citizens of the United States. But given our requirement to be able to fight all across the conflict spectrum to achieve a wide range of policy goals, we must be prepared to support such a vision now and in the future. We must build the capability now for successfully conducting small wars.

Military ways, and specifically air power ways, of achieving policy goals in the third world is the focus of this paper. Military activity is also the focus of our working definition of low-intensity conflict, even though diplomatic, economic, and social aspects of participating in low-intensity conflict may be as important as military activity. Military procedures for designing, procuring, and developing doctrine for new force structures are so time consuming that the Air Force and Department of Defense must begin now to develop the strategies, doctrines, and tactics to ensure effective US participation in the small wars which will become a part of our lives for the foreseeable future.

This paper postulates a role for the Air Force in low-intensity conflict, and suggests ways in which the Air Force can organize and develop resources to support its current DOD responsibility to fight across the entire range of the conflict spectrum, and to suggest ways the Air Force could contribute to supporting future US needs in the area of low-intensity conflict. There are worthwhile lessons to be learned from two historical cases. The first is the British air control experienced in the 1920s and 1930s, which saw air power specifically adapted to controlling what are now called third world countries. A brief look at the history of the USAF Special Air Warfare Center of the 1960s will show what we can learn about early United States Air Force attempts to participate in low-intensity conflicts, especially in the area of counterinsurgency. A case study of modern low-intensity conflict, one in which air power has been playing a key role, will point out in real world terms the difficulties the United States Air Force has in participating in today's small wars. Finally, specific suggestions are made on the philosophic and organizational changes the US Air Force should consider if it is to be a player in low-intensity conflict now and in the future.

NOTES

CHAPTER 1

1. Interview with Gen Wallace H. Nutting, *Newsweek*, 6 June 1983, 24.
2. Sam C. Sarkesian and William L. Scully, eds., *US Policy and Low-Intensity Conflict: Potentials for Military Struggles in the 1980s* (New York: National Defense Information Center, Inc., 1981), 2.
3. Sarkesian and Scully, *US Policy*, 6.
4. Field Manual (FM) 100-20, *Low-Intensity Conflict*, Department of the Army, 16 January 1981, 14-15.
5. Joint Chiefs of Staff (JCS) Pub 1, *Directory of Military and Associated Terms*, Joint Chiefs of Staff, 1 June 1979, 319.
6. Draft JCS Pub 20, vol. 1, 1983, 2-1. (Unclassified)
7. Air Force Manual (AFM) 2-5, *Tactical Air Operations—Special Air Warfare*, Department of the Air Force, 22 June 1965, 19.
8. *Tactical Air Command Manual (TACM) 2-1, Tactical Air Operations*, Headquarters Tactical Air Command, 22 June 1965, 19.
9. AFM 2-5, *Tactical Air Operations—Special Air Warfare*, Department of the Air Force, 10 March 1967, 30.
10. FM 100-20, 14.
11. JCS Pub 1, 1 June 1979, 143.
12. FM 100-20, 14.
13. TACM 2-1, 15 April 1978, 148.
14. JCS Pub 1, 1 June 1979, 273; AFM 1-1, *USAF Basic Doctrine*, Department of the Air Force, 14 February 1979, 22-28; AFM 2-5, 10 March 1967, 20; TACM 2-1, 15 April 1978, 4-54, 4-55.
15. Department of the Air Force, *Air Force 2000* (Washington, D.C.: 11 June 1982), 9 (SECRET). See also W. J. Taylor and S. A. Maaranen, eds., *The Future of Conflict in the 1980s* (Lexington, Mass.: Lexington Books, 1982).
16. Dozens of documents support that conclusion. One of the most recent and carefully researched is W. J. Taylor and R. H. Kupperman, *Strategic Requirements for the Army to the Year 2000*, six volumes (Washington, D.C.: Georgetown Center for Strategic and International Studies, November 1982). See especially volume 2, *The World Environment to the Year 2000*, 3.
17. Richard H. Solomon, ed., *Asian Security in the 1980s: Problems and Policies for a Time of Transition* (Santa Monica, Calif.: Rand Corp., November 1979), 12.

18. Bruce F. Powers, "Is the United States Prepared for Its Most Likely Conflicts?" unpublished Rand paper, February 1981, 5.

19. David Stockman, "Let Chrysler Go Bankrupt," *Washington Post,* 9 December 1979.

20. Remarks by Congressman Newt Gingrich, Air Force Long-Range Planning Conference, Maxwell Air Force Base, Ala., 12 April 1983.

21. David C. Martin, "The Vietnam Syndrome," *Newsweek,* 24 May 1982. Among other things, the Vietnam syndrome makes thinking about, planning for, and participating in counterinsurgency unacceptable to the US military.

22. William J. Taylor, *The Future of Conflict: US Interests,* Washington Paper No. 94 (Washington, D.C.: Georgetown Center for Strategic and International Studies, 1983), 36–38.

CHAPTER 2

AIR POWER IN SMALL WARS: THE BRITISH AIR CONTROL EXPERIENCE

During the 1920s and 1930s the British were very effective in developing a strategy and doctrine for dealing with one form of low-intensity conflict: low-level counterinsurgent warfare. The strategy they developed in the 1920s and 1930s flew in the face of two hundred years of colonial experience because it rejected ground force operations in favor of a new, untried strategy based on air power. The British experience with air control between World Wars I and II demonstrates that air power was once effective in a constabulary and small-war situation. That experience points out how air power, in the hands of creative strategists, can be shaped and applied to support a government's most trying political responsibilities.

Air Control's Genesis

The official British definition of air control circa 1933 noted that political administration of undeveloped countries rests, in the last resort, upon military force. The concept of air control implied that control is applied by aircraft as the primary arm, usually supplemented by forces on the ground, according to particular requirements.[1] How did the Royal Air Force (RAF) come to be the dominant arm in colonial control? What doctrine did they develop to guide operations in the wilds of the empire? What impact did air control have on the development of the Royal Air Force?

British air control resulted from political and military necessity. Emerging victorious but exhausted from the World War I, Britain had to deal with restive populations and disorders of all sorts in its empire. Uprisings against British rule, tribal warfare, and border problems seemed endemic in the Middle East, in Africa, and along India's northwest frontier. The expense of large ground-force expeditions to maintain order in the empire was becoming increasingly burdensome. During the early 1920s the British began to search out alternatives to these costly expeditions.

At that time the fledgling Royal Air Force, drastically reduced in size following the armistice, was being eyed hungrily for absorption by the senior services, which had never really approved the creation of a new service from their air arms.[2] Thus, the RAF faced both a threat and an opportunity—the threat was to its very existence and originated in the postwar struggle for resources between the three services; the opportunity was to develop a better way to control and administer the empire. The challenge, then, was to make itself indispensable to the country as a separate unified service. Since the only immediate requirement for military force was in the colonies, the Royal Air Force needed to develop the methods and means whereby its aircraft could be used as a cheap, effective force to control the empire.

The first indication that the British air force could deal effectively with a colonial disturbance was the successful operation of Z unit in British Somaliland in 1920 against Mohammed bin Abdullah Hassan, the "Mad Mullah," who had been pillaging the eastern tip of Africa since 1899 and had been evading punitive operations by regular British army units and the Anglo-Egyptian-Sudanese army for more than 15 years.[3] The inability of ground forces to stop the mullah and his dervishes from overrunning the country led to a cabinet decision to use air power against the brigand and his large following.

A self-contained RAF expedition, code-named Unit Z, was organized and equipped for a six-month campaign. The unit had 12 de Havilland 9a aircraft, 10 Ford trucks, 2 Ford ambulances, 6 trailers, 2 motorcycles, 2 Crosley light trucks, 36 officers, and 183 men.[4]

By New Year's Day 1920, Z force had built a temporary airdrome at Berbera and was assembling its aircraft, which had been delivered by ship. By 19 January all aircraft had been assembled and flight tested.[5] The RAF's plan was simple: bomb the mullah's forts and pursue his bands wherever they could be found—driving them toward the resident ground forces stationed in the area.

The first raid, carried out by six aircraft, almost ended the war. A bomb blast nearly killed the mullah, but he was saved by a fortuitously placed camel. Further raids, resulting in heavy casualties, took place over the next 2 days causing the dervishes to retreat. Somaliland field forces were positioned to block the retreat while the Royal Air Force switched to a supporting role of maintaining communications between the various ground force detachments, providing air cover, and evacuating wounded. The aircraft proved eminently successful in dislodging the mullah and his followers from their forts and driving them toward the ground forces, which were able to neutralize the mullah and his band of men. The campaign against the mullah lasted only 3 weeks and cost about £ 77,000—a considerable savings over the campaign proposed by the chief of the imperial general staff. He had estimated it would take 12 months and two divisions to do the job, plus an additional expenditure running into millions of pounds to build the railways, roads, and garrison bases necessary to maintain the peace.[6]

The experience in Somaliland showed that there was some justification for Winston Churchill's declaration in December 1919, that "the first duty of the RAF is to garrison the British Empire."[7] As minister of war and air, he had been behind Air Chief Marshal Hugh M. Trenchard's plan to use air power in Somaliland. By 1920, Churchill had asked Trenchard to plan a much more ambitious project—to control Mesopotamia (Iraq) by air.[8] The British were, at the time, nurturing a new Arab government in Iraq, a government not popular among the Arab tribes populating the country. These tribes seemed totally unimpressed with British-sponsored progressive government, which included rules about taxation and standards of acceptable behavior. In late 1920 a serious rebellion against British rule was in progress; the 80 British and Indian battalions (120,000 troops) garrisoning the country were being hard pressed to maintain order. An additional 15,414 men sent from India were quickly absorbed in trying to control an insurrection of at least 131,000 armed men.[9] The British forces were scattered all over the country, protecting population centers and vulnerable lines of communication. With simultaneous outbreaks of violence in several areas, the British force proved too weak in any single spot to deal effectively with the problem. Even with 63 aircraft working with the army, putting down the 1920 insurrection in Iraq was a costly business: about £ 38 million.[10]

In March 1921, with Iraq still restive and unrest simmering in much of the Arab world, the British held a conference in Cairo to discuss the Middle East situation. Winston Churchill, by then colonial secretary, chaired the meeting, which was attended by all three service chiefs. They decided that Iraq, their biggest trouble spot, was to be placed under the control of the Royal Air Force; the progress made in using air power for colonial control in Somaliland would be developed into an operational concept for the RAF. The army began to withdraw from Iraq during the summer of 1922, leaving behind four battalions of British and Indian troops and three armored car companies. Air Marshal Sir John Salmond was made commander in chief of this force plus eight squadrons of aircraft. He was the first air force officer to have complete military command of a colonial territory.[11]

Salmond's command faced both an internal and external threat. The former involved obstreperous tribes that rejected the central control of King Faisal, the British-sponsored ruler of Iraq; the latter threat consisted of encroachments by Turkish irregular (and some regular) forces concentrated in northeast Iraq that were intent on claiming the Mosul Valley area of Iraq for Turkey. In the early days of air control these problems were dealt with by the rather straightforward method of delivering an ultimatum and then bombing the culprits. But, as the Royal Air Force became more experienced in using aircraft to maintain order in places such as Iran, Somaliland, Aden, the Sudan, India's northwest frontier, Palestine, and Transjordan, the concept of air control became much more sophisticated.

Air Control: From Concept to Doctrine

Before this period, Royal Air Force officers began to amass a substantial body of knowledge on what worked and what did not when using air power to police the empire. By the mid-1930s that knowledge had been codified and was being taught at the RAF Staff College and the Imperial Defence College.[12]

Before air control came onto the scene, the British had been using ground forces to control the empire for generations. Essentially, the British had developed two types of operations: the punitive expedition followed by withdrawing the troops to some centralized base—the so-called burn-and-scuttle technique—and an expedition followed by military occupation. There were many obvious difficulties with the army method of control. Paramount was the expense of mounting and maintaining a large expeditionary force. Because of the cost, expeditions could be sent out only rarely, and then only when the need for action had been demonstrated repeatedly. The aim of those expeditions was to administer a major defeat to discourage further undesirable behavior by forcing guerrilla fighters or nomadic tribesmen to concentrate and face British regiments. Usually the British entered and partially destroyed villages to provoke a major battle with the insurgents. However, these campaigns in distant and often harsh areas were hard on British troops. In addition to other casualties, they often suffered numerous losses from disease. And the desired political effect was often superficial and transitory. As soon as the punitive column withdrew, the chastised offenders would begin planning new activity against established authority.

There were other problems with the army method. The columns of the punitive expeditions took an agonizingly long time to reach their targets. Thus the effect of prompt reprisal for a specific act was lost. Further, if a punitive column became a permanent occupying force, its mere presence often became a cause for friction between the local inhabitants and the occupiers. Clearly, the army approach had little subtlety about it. It involved moving masses of troops, engaging the enemy, crushing him, and occupying his territory. Although subtlety of action is not normally associated with air power, the air control tactics developed by the Royal Air Force included some surprisingly subtle techniques.

The doctrine supporting air control operations was exceedingly pragmatic and provided guidance on both goals and techniques. In speaking to the RAF Staff College in 1936, Wing Commander (later Air Chief Marshal) Saundby repeatedly emphasized that the purpose of air control was "to support the political authorities in their tasks of pacification or administration." Because of the political nature of the goal, political authority had to be supreme in these operations. To be successful, the military commander had to cooperate closely with the relevant political authority: "they must understand each other and appreciate each other's point of view properly."[13]

Since the objective of most air control operations was long-term political stability, pacification, and administration, the techniques for achieving those goals were contrary to the training and natural inclination of most military men, namely, to militarily defeat the enemy. The guiding doctrine for air control operations was that they would cause the enemy to submit with the minimum loss of people and material on both sides. Thus, operations were aimed primarily at the morale of those who were disturbing the peace—not by destroying the people or terrifying them into submission, but by disrupting their normal routines to such an extent that continued hostilities became undesirable. As it turned out, the policy of minimal violence proved much more effective (and much cheaper) than the burn-and-scuttle policy of punitive expeditions by ground forces.

For example, the future leader of the Royal Air Force in World War II, Charles F. A. Portal, wrote about an experience he had in Aden in 1935 that illustrated practical techniques supporting the doctrinal precept of minimal violence.[14] His application of air control doctrine began when a caravan en route to Aden from Yemen was raided by the Quteibis tribe in the mountains north of the port of Aden. Portal drafted an ultimatum that was straightforward enough: Pay a fine for damages incurred and hand over the raiders. It then stated the consequences for not complying with the ultimatum:

> If you do not produce the fine and the men, you must leave all your villages and fields, taking all your property and animals with you, and keep right away until the Government gives you permission to come back. The Government will do this as soon as you have complied with the terms. Until you have complied with the terms, your villages and fields may be bombed or fired on at any time by day or night, and you are particularly warned not to touch any bombs that do not go off, as if you do so you will probably get killed.[15]

The last section of the ultimatum outlined the concept of an "inverted blockade," which became the standard method for dealing with similar situations elsewhere in the empire.

The air blockade in this case went on for two months. The tribe went through three phases of behavior during the blockade. At first, it was excited and boastful, shooting freely at the airplanes; next came a period of internal squabbling; and, finally, the tribe's members showed signs of boredom as they stayed away from their homes and fields and grew concerned about getting their crops planted. The tribe's leaders then began to make peace overtures to the government. Portal noted that the most remarkable aspect of this air control operation was the way the tribe came back under government jurisdiction with practically no ill-will, a phenomenon that had also had been observed in India and Iraq. The reason for this, at least in part, was the relatively few casualties that resulted from the operation. In Portal's words:

> It would be the greatest mistake to believe that a victory which spares the lives and feelings of the losers need be any less permament or salutary than one which inflicts heavy losses on the fighting men and results in a peace dictated on a stricken field.[16]

The Requirements of British Air Control

From experience, the British learned that, in applying air power to a specific situation, their air forces had to satisfy certain operational requirements to attain a satisfactory political solution by the minimum use of force. These requirements, of necessity, became critical tenets in the British doctrine of air control. Foremost among these was the need to have a detailed knowledge of the culture, leaders, method of living, and state of mind of the target people. This intelligence was necessary for early warnings of brewing trouble. When action had to be taken, this intelligence made it a great deal simpler to determine the decisive points at which to apply pressure.

Excellent intelligence also enabled the Royal Air Force to avoid attacking people not directly involved—an important requirement in a constabulary-type operation. The Royal Air Force had its own well-trained intelligence officers and civilian political officers on hand to build the necessary intelligence networks.[17] The Royal Air Force required them to become expert in their area of responsibility and to maintain the "closest possible touch with tribes and tribal leaders and with their social and political activities."[18]

To disseminate this intelligence effectively required a well-organized and efficient communications system. During the air control era, the British made good use of wireless telegraphy sets to keep intelligence and political officers in the field in constant touch with the air staff headquarters and higher-level political authorities. One drawback of wireless communication, even in the 1920s and 1930s, was the problem of shifting the responsibility for action from the man in the field to higher level decision makers at home. One of the doctrinal tenets of air control was that the authority to act must be delegated to the on-the-scene commander.[19] The Royal Air Force had learned that procrastination in acting had often been interpreted by recalcitrant tribes as weakness by the government. Good intelligence, effective communications, and the authority to act enabled RAF commanders to deal with trouble at its earliest stages and greatly increased the likelihood of success in air control operations.

Writers of British air control doctrine also provided guidance on dealing with the enemy throughout a campaign. A prime requirement, at the outset, was establishing clearly understood terms. The British made sure that tribal leaders and as many tribesmen as possible understood why the government was taking action and knew exactly what they had to do before the government would end the operation. The British took care to ensure that it was a simple matter for the tribesmen to submit to the will of the government. Not only did the British maintain constant contact with the enemy throughout a campaign, but they also delivered propaganda by airborne loudspeaker. This propaganda emphasized the peaceful intent of the British demands and stressed the futility of resistance against the impersonal, invulnerable, and ubiquitous air force. Psychological warfare was tailored to create a sense of helplessness among the target people and was an integral part of air control operations. Coupled with the inverted blockade, psychological warfare proved useful in air control operations.

A final aspect of British air control operations built upon the overriding principle of minimal violence. After a successful air control campaign, it was essential to use the aircraft as a means of positive contact with the former enemy, doctors were flown to remote sites when needed, natives were evacuated to large medical facilities if required, messages were delivered from one local chief to another in the course of normal flying duties, and similar acts of good faith were performed. This type of humanitarian work helped enormously in reintegrating formerly rebellious tribes back into the fold of law-abiding citizens and showed them some benefits that could result by accepting British control.[20]

Air Control and Today's US Air Force

Most who have looked at the British experience with air control have concluded that the simple applications of that concept are gone forever.[21] Technology and the arms bazaar can provide even the smallest insurgent group with sophisticated surface-to-air missiles and antiaircraft artillery. Clearly, the nearly unchallenged operating environment enjoyed by the British in their pre-World War II empire no longer exists. And because US public opinion is deeply concerned about another Vietnam disaster, any discussion on applying US power in small wars is very unpopular. In spite of those obvious limiting technical and political factors, the US Air Force can learn from Britain's air control experience.

Perhaps the most important lesson we can extract from this episode in the history of the Royal Air Force is that air power can be shaped in creative ways to achieve political results. The methods used by the British to achieve simple solutions were not all that simple, at least as the doctrine involved grew with experience. A very sophisticated combination of superb intelligence, communications, and psychological warfare coupled with a judicious application of firepower was necessary to achieve the desired results: pacification of a troubled colonial area with minimum violence, lasting results, and minimum cost. To design such a program required a flexibility of thinking that was most impressive. Airmen emerging from World War I with their experience of fleets of aircraft being used for bombing and air-to-air missions were able to modify their concepts of air power to apply it to a totally new environment with a totally new mission. While they were developing these new concepts, Britain's air officers quickly learned the political nature of military power. They participated in the political process of formulating plans of action that meshed political goals and military capability—training that stood them in good stead during World War II.

Technology of course played a key role in the success of Britain's air control concept. There was a mystique about the aircraft in relation to the people being controlled. The aircraft was seen as an impersonal, invulnerable projection of British power that could overcome physical obstacles quickly and apply firepower with extreme precision. These characteristics made air power in underdeveloped areas an almost irresistible force.

Modern technology may make today's aircraft as effective a weapon for supporting third world friends or pursuing limited military objective in small wars as Britain's de Havilland 9a was for policing the empire in the 1920s and 1930s. Equipped with long-range, highly accurate standoff weapons, modern aircraft could likewise project power quickly and with extreme precision. For instance, it could be in the interests of the United States to assist a friendly country facing a threat of an external foe's sophisticated surface-to-air missiles. Long-range standoff US aircraft could jam or eliminate the SAM threat from positions far from the battlefield. In another scenario, if an aggressive, expansionistic third world nation were to mass troops and equipment on the border of a country the United States wished to support, demonstration of US ability to locate and destroy some of the massed equipment using weapons far beyond the range of the aggressor's defensive systems might prove to be an effective deterrent measure when diplomacy failed to keep the peace. If weapons are ever placed in space, of course, the concept of using precise standoff firepower assumes a much wider dimension. However, the United States needs to have a concept of operations and a doctrine for their use before such space weapons are produced and deployed. Many of the techniques developed by the Royal Air Force for operating in the third world could serve the US Air Force very well as it examines its role in the small wars of today, and in those of the next decade and beyond.

NOTES

CHAPTER 2

1. Great Britain, Royal Air Force Staff Memorandum No. 52, Air Ministry, June 1933, 3.
2. See Great Britain, Cabinet Paper 365(29), "The Fuller Employment of Air Power in Imperial Defence," December 1929, for a brief outline of army-navy attempts to dismember the Royal Air Force from 1919–29.
3. C. G. Grey, *A History of the Air Ministry* (London: Unwin Brothers Ltd., 1940), 173.
4. Flight Lieutenant F. A. Skoulding, "With Z Unit in Somaliland," *The Royal Air Force Quarterly* (July 1931): 390.
5. Ibid., 392.
6. Charles Sims, *The Royal Air Force: The First Fifty Years* (London: Adam and Charles Black, 1963), 38.
7. Ibid., 37.
8. Martin Gilbert, *Winston Churchill: The Stricken World* (Boston: Houghton Mifflin, 1975), 216–18.
9. Flight Lieutenant M. Thomas, "The Royal Air Force in Iraq Since 1918," lecture given at the RAF Staff College, Andover, England, 1923.
10. N. N. Golovine, *Air Strategy* (London: Gae and Polden, Ltd., 1936), 24.
11. Sims, *The Royal Air Force,* 39–40.
12. Air Vice Marshal E. R. Ludow-Hewitt, deputy chief of the air staff, Air Staff Memorandum No. 52 "Air Control," lecture to the Imperial Defence College, London, April 1933; Wing Commander R.H.M.S. Saundby, "Small Wars with Particular Reference to Air Control in Undeveloped Countries," lecture to RAF Staff College, 14th Course, Andover, England, June 1936.
13. Saundby, "Small Wars," 16.
14. Air Commodore Charles F. A. Portal, "Air Force Cooperation in Policing the Empire," *Royal United Service Institution Journal* (May 1937): 341–58.
15. Ibid., 352.
16. Ibid., 354.
17. For an eminently readable example of how the Royal Air Force developed and used intelligence in an air control operation, see Glubb, *War in the Desert: An R.A.F. Frontier Campaign* (London: Hodder and Stoughton, 1960).
18. Saundby, "Small Wars," 20.
19. Ibid., 6.
20. Portal, "Air Force Cooperation," 356–57.
21. See Lt Col Bryce Poe II, "The Role of Aerospace Attack Weapons in International Affairs," (Paper for the National War College, Washington, D.C., 1965).

CHAPTER 3

THE MOROCCO-POLISARIO WAR: A CASE STUDY OF A MODERN LOW-INTENSITY CONFLICT

The Kingdom of Morocco has been fighting a persistent guerrilla enemy, the Polisario, for almost 10 years. Polisario is an acronym for the Popular Front for the Liberation of Saguia el Hamra and Rio de Oro. This war brings together several elements that may suggest the nature of future low-intensity conflicts: nationalist ambitions (in this case where there is no nation), massive external support, complicated political motivations on the part of both the combatants and their sponsors, regional competition, sophisticated weapons in the hands of small, irregular guerrilla formations, and the potential involvement of the superpowers. It is a little-publicized war that is poorly understood in the United States and involves one of America's oldest friends. King Hassan II, very much the ruler of Morocco, has always been pro-Western in his political inclination and in recent years has made a strong move toward increasing his ties with the United States. The Reagan administration, in need of secure air base facilities to support possible Mideast operations, has been courting Hassan and has sent an ambassador to Rabat to assure the monarch that "he can count on us."[1] How Hassan interprets this commitment by the United States to support his regime both economically and militarily in its effort against the Polisario is difficult to assess. But there can be no doubt that in return for access to Moroccan air bases, Hassan will expect a military and economic quid pro quo.

Resources and Topography of Western Sahara

The war between Morocco and the Polisario is over sovereignty of one of the least hospitable areas in the world: Western Sahara. A former Spanish colony known as the Spanish Sahara from 1884 to 1976, this region stretches some 430 miles from the southern border of Morocco to the northern border of Mauritania.

Western Sahara is divided into two regions: the northern panhandle, Saguia el Hamra, and the larger southern area called Rio de Oro. Together the two regions form an area about the size of Colorado—an area of vast empty space, rough terrain, few people, and quite modest resources.

Perhaps the most striking feature of Western Sahara's topography is that the sand dunes one normally associates with the Sahara Desert are not the dominant land form. There are sandy areas scattered throughout Western Sahara and sand dunes are prevalent along the coast, but most of the area consists of rocky plains with escarpments rising to several hundred feet.[2] This rocky desert floor makes rapid motor vehicle transport possible, contrary to the image one normally has of laborious movement over seemingly endless sand dunes. This terrain has been a key factor in the success of Polisario operations over the past eight years.

The desert of Western Sahara has enough water sources to support seasonal grazing by the camels and goats belonging to the handful of Bedouins who have roamed the borderless stretches of desert included in southern Morocco, Algeria, Mauritania, and Western Sahara for generations immemorial. All borders in this vast area are the artificial creations of former colonial powers, borders that have been meaningless to peoples unacquainted with Western concepts of nationalism and frontiers.

Within these spaces there is little of economic value. Virtually all the writing on the war in the Sahara describes the areas as the "mineral-rich former Spanish colony." It is true that there are considerable high-grade phosphate deposits in Western Sahara. In the early 1960s the Spanish reported that about 1.7 billion tons of phosphate rock were located in the Bu-Craâ region southeast of El Ayoun, the largest city in the Sahara. However, Morocco proper has deposits of 16.2 billion tons of phosphate rock—eight times the deposits of Western Sahara, or about one-half the total world reserves of 34.5 billion tons.[3] Currently, Morocco is the third largest producer (after the United States and the USSR) but the world's largest exporter of phosphates. Its phosphate reserves are more than sufficient to continue to bring in nearly $700 million per year in foreign exchange far into the future. That $700 million is an important but by no means dominant portion of Morocco's $17.5-billion gross national product. Unlike other Arab countries whose economies rely on one natural resource such as gas or oil, Morocco is diversified enough that phosphates are not the alpha and omega of its economy. Phosphates, then, seem to be an exaggerated factor in Morocco's decision to fight a long and expensive war in the Sahara. Similarly, other mineral resources do not seem to enter the picture as causes of the war. Although some iron deposits have been found in the Sahara, they do not qualify as commercial quantities of iron ore, and other mineral and oil deposits have yet to be found. The rich fishing grounds off the Atlantic coast of the Sahara are an important potential resource that has not yet been fully exploited. If the mineral wealth of Western Sahara is marginal, then why have the Moroccans and the Polisario been so persistent in their conflict?

Moroccan Claims and Stakes in Western Sahara

Moroccans have emotional and political claims to the Spanish Sahara. They also have historical arguments to justify their claim to the Sahara, but these are less telling than the emotion that has been generated by the Moroccan populace at all levels. Historically, Morocco traces its lineage from the Almoravid and Almohad Berber empires, which, in the 11th century, began a process that led to an empire stretching from southern Spain to Senegal. Thus, Morocco has irredentist claims to a vast territory that includes, besides Western Sahara, all of Mauritania and parts of Algeria and Mali—the so-called Greater Morocco. As Lewis B. Ware has pointed out, however, Morocco's historical claims to the Sahara are open to serious question, and by following Moroccan historical analysis to its logical conclusion, Mauritania emerges as the country with the best historic argument for owning Western Sahara.[4]

The idea of Greater Morocco has a good deal of emotional appeal among Moroccan nationalists, but pursuing it is unrealistic. On the one hand, except for the Algerian-Moroccan boundary in the Tindouf region, the borders of Mauritania, Western Sahara, Mali, and Algeria are well defined (fig. 4). On the other hand, the nomadic nature of the herding tribes of North Africa makes political boundaries irrelevant to the question of sovereignty in the context of the Sahara.

A stronger, more relevant basis on which Morocco can and does justify its claims to the region is the tribal allegiances and strong Islamic religious bonds that have existed between the Moroccan sultan and the Sahrawi tribes that have roamed Western Sahara. Traditionally, in Islamic cultures, tribes have conferred sovereignty on their rulers by a pledge of allegiance—bai'a.[5] Most of the Saharan tribes over the past two hundred years have sworn allegiance to the sultan of Morocco, who, as Commander of the Faithful, combines both religious and political authority in his being.[6] This allegiance, the Moroccans argue, carries the same weight as territorial sovereignty in non-Islamic, Western civilizations. Administrative control of these tribes was not always feasible. There were no population centers to control and the sultan was not usually able to project his power continuously into the far reaches of the desert areas. The allegiance of these tribes allowed the sultan to establish a measure of sovereignty over the region without compelling him to have absolute control over each tribe and the land it inhabited. The pattern of historical and indirect political control over the Sahrawi tribes provides Morocco with a reasonable basis for laying claim to Western Sahara.

Modern Moroccans care little for the specific historical and legal claims their country has over Western Sahara. Since independence in 1956, Moroccans from all parts of the political spectrum have agreed that the Sahara is part of Morocco.

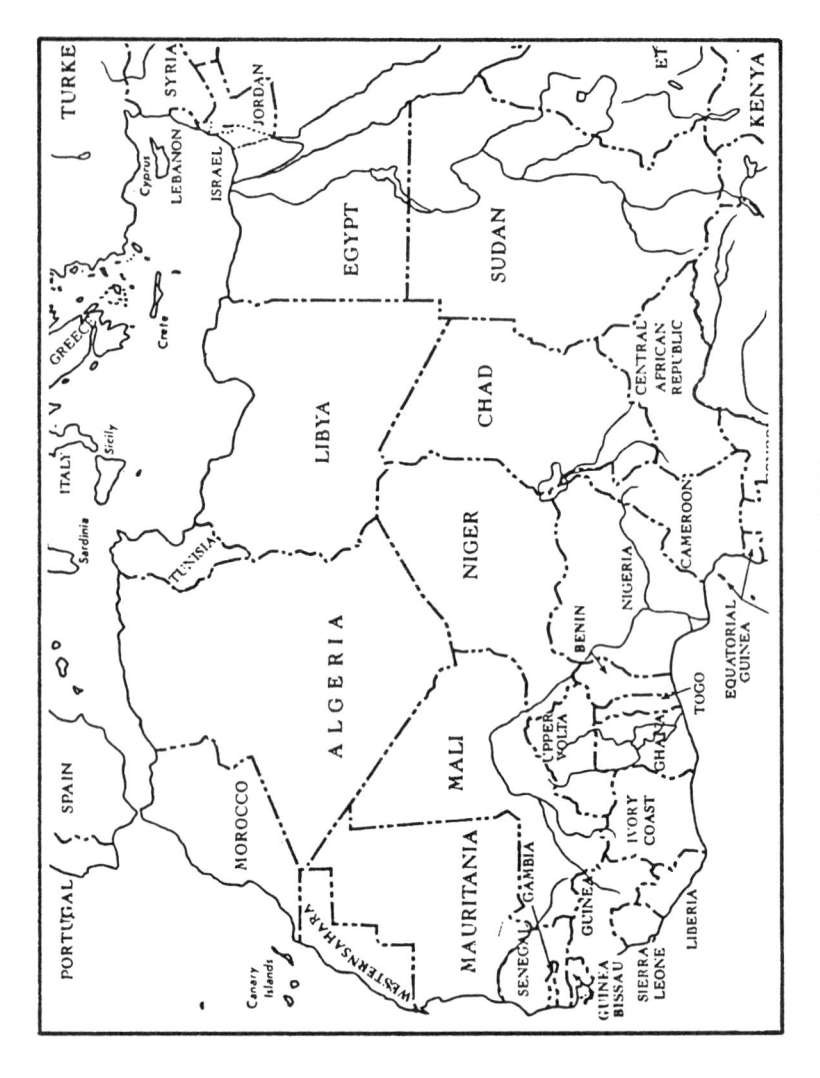

Figure 4. North Africa.

The conservative and nationalist Istiqlal party pushed Moroccan claims for the Sahara at the time of independence. Two years later King Mohammed V, the father of the current monarch, committed the regime to "recovering" Western Sahara.

Morocco worked diligently in the diplomatic arena to establish its claim over Western Sahara. During the 1960s this effort focused primarily on improving the relationships between Rabat, Algiers, and Nouakchott. In 1970, after settling other problems (Morocco and Algeria signed a 20-year Treaty of Solidarity and Cooperation in 1969, and in 1970 Morocco signed a friendship treaty with Mauritania that ended any Moroccan claim to Mauritanian territory), these three countries began to discuss issues relating to the future of the Sahara. In the early 1970s, Morocco, Algeria, and Mauritania applied coordinated pressure to convince Spain to decolonize the Sahara. Previously Spanish movement toward that end had been fitful and halting at best.

This joint movement lasted until 1974, when Morocco rejected the option of an independent Saharan state and actively began to assert its own claim to the Sahara. Morocco pressed its case in the United Nations, where the International Court of Justice was asked to provide an advisory opinion on the legal status of the Saharan territory prior to its colonization by Spain in 1884. The court's task was to determine if the Sahara belonged to any nation when it was colonized by Spain and to evaluate any legal ties linking Western Sahara with Morocco.

The court rendered its advisory opinion in October 1975. The judges decided unanimously that when Spain colonized the Sahara the territory was not without a master. The court concluded that Morocco did have legal ties of allegiance with the Saharan tribes, but these legal ties did not constitute Moroccan sovereignty over the area. The court stated the rights of the Sahrawi population to self-determination. Morocco, however, chose to interpret the advisory opinion as an endorsement of the kingdom's position, equating the court's finding of legal ties to the Sahara with territorial sovereignty. The parts of the opinion that did not support Morocco were ignored.[7]

King Hassan used the decision of the International Court of Justice as support for Morocco's claim to the Sahara. The court's opinion was followed in quick order by the so-called Green March. Just after the decision, King Hassan announced that 350,000 civilians, armed only with their Korans, would march from Morocco into the Sahara to reclaim the territory. King Hassan's proposal won the enthusiastic support of all Moroccans; it was a nonviolent step to force Spain into moving forward on negotiations to decolonize Spanish Sahara.

By this time (late 1975) Spain, concerned over the succession to Generalissimo Franco and by a Morocco poised to peacefully invade the Sahara, wanted only to get out of the territory without disgrace. As the Green March began to develop a life and a force of its own, Moroccan-Spanish negotiations forged ahead. On 6 November, the mass of Green Marchers crossed the frontier of Western Sahara. By 9 November Spain had agreed to settle the Saharan question with Morocco and Mauritania, excluding the "interested" Algerians. This development led to the November 1975 tripartite agreement between Morocco, Mauritania, and Spain whereby Spain was to transfer administrative authority (not sovereignty) to a joint Moroccan-Mauritanian administration. Spain quickly withdrew its troops and administrators; Morocco filled the vacuum. Morocco and Mauritania then partitioned the Sahara. The struggle began with Mauritania and Morocco on one side and the Polisario Front, backed by Algeria, on the other.

The Polisario Front

The Polisario's origins, composition, and leadership are difficult to pinpoint. The organization was formed in 1973 at Nouakchott, Mauritania, and first fought Spanish troops that same year.[8] The Polisario claims to be the legitimate representative of the Sahrawi people striving to establish an independent nonaligned state from the territory colonized by Spain. It has established a government in exile, the Saharan Arab Democratic Republic (SADR), in Algiers, with its center of strength being the large base camp near Tindouf in southwestern Algeria. The SADR defines itself as a democratic socialist republic with Islam as its state religion within the recognized borders of Saguia el Hamra and Rio de Oro.

The Polisario was initially based in Mauritania and for two years—1973 to 1975—fought the Spanish in a series of harassment operations. During that period relations between Morocco, Mauritania, and the Polisario were friendly. That situation changed as it became clear that Spain would partition its colony between Morocco and Mauritania without really considering the desires of the Sahrawi people. Following the division and occupation of Spanish Sahara by Morocco and Mauritania, the Polisario organized an exodus of Sahrawis out of the territory to the camps of Tindouf.

The number of "legitimate" Sahrawis, that is, those who could be considered actual residents of Western Sahara versus the total number of refugees living in the Tindouf area, is even more nebulous than the Polisario's origins. The Spanish census of 1974 showed a total of 73,497 Sahrawis.[9] The 25,000 to 30,000 Sahrawis who left the territory for Morocco in the 1950s should also be included in this total. Thus the "true" Sahrawi population is perhaps a bit over 100,000 people. At Tindouf the nationalities and the number of refugees are subject to serious debate. Morocco claims that only 15,000 Sahrawis are in the camps and that these are outnumbered by refugees from all over north and central Africa. Relief agencies have estimated from 40,000 to 100,000 refugees in the camps; the Polisario claims a camp population of 100,000 to 150,000. John Damis, a leading analyst and writer on Western Sahara, made a count of tents in the camps in 1979 and found a range of 17,000 to 35,000 refugees in the camps.[10]

Whatever the movement's size may be, the leadership of the Polisario—a combination of Moroccan- and Spanish-educated Western Saharan nationalists, Moroccans, and Mauritanians—has highly politicized the people in the camps. A central goal of the Polisario's leaders is to develop a sense of loyalty to a nation—the Saharan Arab Democratic Republic—among a people whose loyalty has been to families and tribes. Reports from journalists suggest that the camps at Tindouf are well organized and produce a high level of political awareness among the residents.[11] The movement has been fighting the Moroccans for more than nine years now and has suffered significant losses; still its leaders have been able to replace fighters and maintain cohesion among the Tindouf refugees with little apparent difficulty. This fact suggests a considerable degree of success in their organizational and administrative methods even though some Polisario defectors have reported that recruitment is done by promises of money and food and that discipline in the camps is maintained by intimidation.[12]

In spite of its strong leadership and its apparent cohesiveness, the Polisario could not survive without the continuous support of Algeria and other countries. Algeria provides territorial sanctuaries, food, military aid, and diplomatic support; Libya provides substantial arms supplies; and Cuba, North Vietnam, East Germany, and North Korea give some training to the Polisario forces.[13] The Polisario would like the world to view the struggle as the Sahrawi people's struggle for self-determination against the Moroccan invaders and occupiers. But the interest of such worldwide destabilizers as Cuba and Libya, the extensive involvement of Algeria (which may even be described as control), and the motley composition of the Polisario suggests a much more complex picture than that of Moroccan aggressors trampling on home-grown Sahrawi nationalists.

Algeria

Even though not an active combatant in the Saharan conflict, Algeria is a key player. In 1975, Algeria switched from supporting Morocco and Mauritania, which had been pressing Spain to recognize Moroccan-Mauritanian claims to the colony, to insisting on self-determination for Western Sahara. Algeria had come to realize that its long-term geopolitical interests conflicted with a Moroccan-dominated Sahara. Ideologically, Algeria supports national liberation movements and the principle of self-determination. These ideological commitments fit very nicely with supporting the Polisario against a traditional, conservative, pro-Western Moroccan monarchy.

In a sense Algeria may be using the Polisario to wage a surrogate war that is very costly to the Moroccans. A Moroccan-controlled Sahara would contribute to Morocco's challenge to Algerian preeminence in the Maghreb (Morocco, Algeria, Tunisia, and Libya) and, by extending Morocco's borders far to the south, would tend to "encircle" Algeria. The Algerians clearly would like to avoid such developments. The Polisario's activities effectively tie down the bulk of Morocco's armed forces and are a serious financial drain on the weak Moroccan economy. The level of financial support to keep the Polisario operating and to maintain the base camps at Tindouf is a pittance for Algiers.

Algeria also has an economic interest in the Sahara. Large iron ore deposits exist in southwest Algeria, but to exploit these deposits Algeria must be able to transport the ore to processing plants. The best way to do this is to haul the ore by rail to the Atlantic coast of Morocco or the Sahara. An independent (Algerian-dominated) Saharan state would make exploitation of this iron feasible and perhaps would lead to joint exploitation of the resource. However, Morocco and Algeria—as regional competitors and, currently, implacable enemies—may find it difficult, if not impossible, to work out arrangements for transporting the ore across Morocco for export from the Atlantic coast.

Both Algeria and Morocco have been ambiguous and contradictory in their statements regarding the Saharan problem. Algeria claims to have supported self-determination in the Sahara since the mid-1960s. Yet, Algeria's President Boumediene agreed, in both 1974 and 1975, to let Morocco and Mauritania take over Western Sahara.[14] However, in late 1975 Algeria had become vehemently opposed to Morocco and Mauritania's takeover of Spanish Sahara. Meanwhile, Morocco had supported Sahrawi self-determination between 1966 and 1974. But in mid-1974 King Hassan opposed a referendum that could have led to Saharan independence. Since then, and especially since 1979 when Mauritania withdrew from the conflict, Hassan has considered the Sahara as Moroccan and has acted accordingly. One major difference between the Moroccan and the Algerian positions exists, however. In Morocco every level of the population and every shade of political opinion fully supports Hassan's efforts to regain and keep the Sahara. But, while a general feeling exists in Algeria that the Polisario's goals are just, most Algerians would be unwilling to make the same kind of sacrifices in men and treasure to support the Polisario that the Moroccans have made and continue to make to support their government's goals in the Sahara.

Mauritania

Mauritania has had a difficult time with the Saharan conflict and has had wild policy shifts over the past several years. Mauritania obtained the Tiris al Gharbiyya area of Western Sahara in the tripartite agreement with Spain and Morocco in 1975. Because Mauritania began its occupation of the southern Sahara with a weak military capability (12,000 troops in its army) and a vast, empty northern border area to patrol, it relied on military assistance from Morocco and financial aid from Saudi Arabia to fight the Polisario. Additionally, there was almost no popular support to keep up the fight. In the end the struggle was too expensive for the Mauritanians. In August 1979, they signed a peace agreement with the Polisario, withdrew their forces, and abandoned any claim to the Western Sahara.

Mauritania's withdrawal from the conflict, coupled with its inability to control incursions from its northern border area into Western Sahara, has strained relations with Morocco considerably in the past few years. Relations between the two had never been especially good, indeed they had begun on an unfavorable note. When Mauritania was granted independence by France in 1960, Morocco refused to recognize Mauritania's sovereignty; Morocco considered Mauritania as part of Greater Morocco. In 1969 Morocco finally recognized Mauritania's existence, but Mauritania remained suspicious of Moroccan ambitions and considered the Western Sahara a useful buffer against Moroccan expansion.

To complicate matters further, Mauritania's Saharan policy has shifted often over the years. From 1960 to 1974 Mauritania supported self-determination by referendum for the Sahara, believing that the ethnic closeness of the Sahrawis and the Mauritanians would result in a Sahrawi federation with Mauritania. Even if the Western Sahara became an independent state, it would be a buffer to Morocco. In 1974–75, when it became clear that Morocco was going to take the Sahara either by peaceful or violent action, Mauritania considered dividing the Sahara between the two countries as an acceptable outcome. This decision, which seemed to be a good way of preventing Morocco from expanding to Mauritania's northern border, forced Mauritania into a costly war with the Polisario. It ended when the Ould Daddah government was overthrown by a military coup in July 1978.

Since making peace with the Polisario in 1979, Mauritania has tried not to antagonize either Morocco or Algeria, but it has not been very successful in avoiding conflict with Morocco. The two countries broke diplomatic relations in March 1981 over alleged Moroccan complicity in a coup attempt in Nouakchott.[15] Moreover, the Polisario, in 1981, was operating freely in the undefended and unoccupied wastes of northern Mauritania. In response, Moroccan air force fighters have on several occasions attacked Polisario base camps in Mauritania. And even though diplomatic relations between Morocco and Mauritania resumed in June 1981 after Saudi Arabia mediated the dispute, the situation between the two countries has remained cool.

Libya

Libya, under the revolutionary guidance of Colonel Mu'ammar Qadhafi, has been a strong supporter of the Polisario. Qadhafi's personal dislike of Hassan II (who is, in Qadhafi's eyes, an anachronistic reactionary) is probably an important factor in Libya's Western Saharan policy.

Libya was a financial backer and arms supplier to the Polisario from 1973 to 1985, when Libyan backing was stopped following the conclusion of the Oujda

Accord. This arrangement has led to an uneasy relationship between Libya and Algeria, the Polisario's other main backer. Algeria tends to exert a moderating influence over the Polisario, preferring to drain Morocco's resources rather than engage Morocco in open conflict, while Libya encourages a radical and violent path for the Polisario even at the risk of direct hostilities with Morocco.[16] Algeria is also leery of the level of Libyan influence over the Polisario. Some observers have reported that Algerian and Libyan factions have formed within the Polisario, which could result in a conflict over the strategy, tactics, and methods that the Polisario will adopt as the struggle with Morocco continues.

France

France, a power in African events, has maintained a neutral stance on Western Sahara, recognizing neither Moroccan sovereignty in the Sahara nor the Polisario. France provides economic and military assistance to Morocco and is Morocco's most important trading partner. Overall, France tilts toward Morocco and against Algeria and Libya in the Sahara dispute.

France's heaviest involvement in the conflict occurred following two incidents in 1977. In the first incident in May, the Polisario kidnapped six French civilians from the Mauritanian mining center at Zouirat and killed two others. The second incident came in October, when the Polisario took two French railway technicians as prisoners. In December, the French successfully used air power stationed in Dakar, Senegal to obtain the release of these hostages.[17]

With the election of Mitterand as president in May 1981, France seems to have become "more" neutral in its Saharan position. Former President Giscard d'Estaing and King Hassan were close personal friends, a relationship the King does not enjoy with Mitterand. Since US-Moroccan relations are warming quickly, France's importance to Morocco as a source of military supplies and assistance may be reduced.

The United States

For many years the United States has maintained a neutral stance on the Saharan issue. We have recognized Moroccan administrative control over the Sahara but not its sovereignty over the area. However, the election of the Reagan administration, the assignment of Joseph Verner Reed as ambassador to Morocco, and the need to obtain US air basing rights in Morocco to support Mideast military contingencies have led to significant changes in the United States position over the past five years.

The United States has long been an important source of military hardware for Morocco. Most of the purchases made during the 1970s were designed to modernize the Moroccan military and were not related to the Saharan conflict. In

1977, however, Rabat asked Washington for OV-10 and F-5E fixed-wing aircraft and Cobra attack helicopters for use in Western Sahara. Previous US-Moroccan agreements stipulated that US-supplied weapons could be used only for internal security and self-defense.[18] Morocco had been using previously obtained F-5A and B aircraft in the Sahara since 1976, a fact used by the Carter administration to justify its rejection of the Hassan regime's request for additional arms.

In 1979 the Carter administration began to shift its policy regarding Moroccan arms purchases. The Polisario had made several attacks inside Morocco proper, causing the administration to reconsider the nature of the war itself. A feeling in the government that the United States had not done enough to support the Shah of Iran also contributed to Washington's decision to be more supportive of Hassan II. By October 1979 the Carter administration had approved the sale of 6 OV-10s, 20 F-5Es, and 24 Hughes Model 500 helicopters to Morocco. Financing was provided by Saudi Arabia. Under President Carter the US government linked these arms sales to Moroccan efforts to "progress in negotiations."[19]

The Reagan administration has dropped any conditions in supporting the Moroccans.[20] The need for aircraft basing rights, the recognition of Morocco's strategic position, and the strong desire to demonstrate dependable US support of our friends has formed the basis for new bonds of friendship between the United States and Moroccan governments. Ambassador Reed has been fervent in his public statements, telling King Hassan and the Moroccan people to "count on us; we are with you." His analysis that "it is obvious that the next pressure point for the Soviets is going to be the Kingdom of Morocco, situated strategically as it is on the Straits of Gibraltar" adds to the Moroccan perception that the United States has security interests which involve Morocco very strongly.[21] Clearly, this development puts a new emphasis on Morocco that has been missing from US policy in years past.

Peripheral Players

Several players, although not directly involved with the war in the Sahara, nevertheless have an interest in it. United States policy must consider these peripheral players in the Saharan situation because of larger regional and international issues that could be affected by US actions in the Western Sahara.

The USSR

Moscow has remained aloof from the Saharan conflict. The Soviets are of course the ultimate source for the Polisario's arms, but financing and distributing those arms to the Polisario seem to be controlled by Libya and Algeria. The political compatibility of Moscow and Algiers provides the Soviets with a needed doorway through which to involve themselves in North Africa. Yet at the same time, Moscow and Rabat have entered into a multibillion-dollar phosphate deal as well as a major fishing agreement.[22] Moscow may be positioning itself in anticipation that a revolutionary regime someday will replace King Hassan. At present the USSR wants good relations with both Morocco and Algeria and is remarkably restrained in supporting or even having contact with the Polisario Front.

Saudi Arabia

Saudi Arabia strongly supports King Hassan. Hassan, as a direct descendent of Mohammed, has considerable prestige as Commander of the Faithful, and, thus, is a central figure in modern Islam. The Saudis provide massive financing (perhaps $1 billion a year) to support Morocco's war in the desert and play a key role in mediating disputes among the Arab nations of North Africa. The importance of Saudi Arabia to the United States also lends clout to its effort to influence events in North Africa.

Spain

Spain is strictly neutral in the Saharan conflict and has not recognized the Saharan Arab Democratic Republic. Spain has important economic links to Morocco and is willing to help find a solution to the situation. At present, however, Spanish influence in the situation is negligible. Moreover, the two Spanish enclaves in Morocco—Ceuta and Melilla—provide a basis for occasional friction between the two countries.

The War's Importance

The international implications of the war in the Sahara are readily apparent from the foregoing and are well documented in the literature dealing with that conflict. However, the war itself and the tactics both sides are developing as the fighting continues are not particularly well known. The relative unconcern of most governments with this remote and comparatively small war, the dearth of reliable reporting from the war zone, and the seemingly interminable length of the Saharan war all contribute to its relegation far down on the list of problems facing the world's nations. Yet, this war offers some very important lessons on the use of air power, the role of defensive thinking in strategy, and the impact of superpower assistance on third world armed forces. The United States must learn these lessons if it expects to be able to participate effectively in the small wars that might occur during the remainder of this century, especially in Africa, Asia, and Central and South America.

This analysis examines the pattern of the Saharan war through the prism of the Royal Moroccan Air Force (RMAF) experience.[23] This approach may seem incongruous since the RMAF is so much smaller and less influential within Morocco than the ground forces of the Forces Armees Royales (FAR). Today's Moroccan air force has about 13,000 people compared to about 130,000 in the ground forces, yet it plays a key role in every phase of this desert war. The Royal Moroccan Air Force has set the pace for the conflict. Its actions have at times denied the Polisario fighters the freedom of movement so critical to their success and have led the Polisario to obtain high-technology weapons to drive the Moroccan air force from the battlefield.

Evolution of the War

Many political and military benchmarks mark the ebb and flow of this long and at times spasmodic war. Looking at it from the Moroccan perspective, the war can be seen as developing in four phases: static defense (November 1975 to June 1979), incipient offense (July 1979 to September 1981), SA-6-induced paralysis (October to December 1981), and aftermath of Guelta Zemmour (January 1982 to present).

Static Defense (November 1975 to June 1979)

The Morocco-Polisario conflict can be said to have begun with the Green March on 6 November 1975 when 350,000 unarmed Moroccan civilians entered the Spanish Sahara and reclaimed it for Morocco. The Moroccan army organized, supported, and controlled the Green March and remained in Saharan cities and outposts after the Green Marchers withdrew. Meanwhile the Polisario moved many Sahrawis out of the Western Sahara and into the base camp in Tindouf, Algeria. Polisario strength increased rapidly from about 800 to 3,000. Perhaps 2,000 to 2,500 of the new Polisario fighters came from the Spanish Sahara territorial police, "nomadic troops," and former members of the regular Spanish army in the Sahara, mostly local Saharans. These men brought to the Front their training, knowledge of the terrain, and weapons.[24]

From late 1975 through mid-1976, the Polisario tried to prevent Morocco and Mauritania from establishing military and political control over the Sahara. At first the Polisario attempted to hold towns and engage Moroccan units in fixed battles. Moroccan superiority in numbers and firepower soon forced the Polisario to adopt more productive, conventional guerrilla hit-and-run tactics. The value of firepower, however, was a lesson the Polisario learned thoroughly, and using firepower with devastating effect has become an important factor in their operations.

In 1976 and 1977 Morocco was clearly on the defensive, the Polisario on the offensive. Moroccan strategy concentrated on maintaining control of the few principal population centers and oases. The guerrillas, well supported by Algeria, struck at will in the Sahara and northern Mauritania. Polisario tactics at this time emphasized small unit actions (five to eight land rovers loaded with men), mobility, and surprise. Essentially these rebel units harassed Moroccan and Mauritanian forces, interdicted supplies, and occasionally ambushed government patrols.

By 1977 the Polisario had improved its ability to coordinate military operations and could bring motorized columns of up to 150 vehicles to bear on an objective. In the spring of 1977, for example, the Front was able to attack the Mauritanian mining down of Zouirat from two directions and to mass firepower equal to a Moroccan regiment.[25] The Polisario was clearly concentrating its efforts on Mauritania, a country tottering on the brink of economic collapse, to force Mauritania to withdraw from its partnership with Morocco in the Sahara. The war was a key factor in the July 1978 coup in Nouakchott, which saw Mokhtar Ould Daddah replaced by a military junta. Militarily, Mauritania was no longer a factor in the war after July 1978, and in 1979 the junta withdrew all Mauritanian claims to Western Sahara and made peace with the Polisario.

During this phase of the war, the Moroccan air force was basically ineffective in fighting the Polisario. The only area in which it was effective was aerial resupply. The Polisario's ability to harass and interdict ground transport at will made resupply by air vital in the early part of the war. The Royal Moroccan Air Force accomplished this important, and often overlooked, mission of supplying Moroccan ground forces in the cities and remote garrisons with its fleet of C-130 cargo planes.

The Moroccan fighter force, in comparison, had little experience in ground-air coordination, no routine tactical air intelligence, and limited experience in locating and attacking mobile targets. Although it would react to army requests for support, the Moroccan air force had almost no success in denying the Polisario freedom of movement in the desert. On the one hand, the mainstays of the RMAF's fighter force, Fouga Magisters and T-34s, had limited capabilities. On the other hand, the Moroccans utilized their more advanced aircraft to only a limited extent. Together, all the F-5s flown in the south during 1977 and 1978 averaged only about 100 hours a month (fig. 5). Nonetheless, the RMAF was enough of a threat to the Polisario that SA-7 surface-to-air missiles began to appear in the rebels' inventory of weapons by 1976.[26]

The most interesting use of air power during this period occurred in 1977. Over a period of several months the Polisario struck several targets in Mauritania and in the process killed a French doctor and his wife and captured eight other

Figure 5. F-5—US Supplied Fighter of the Royal Moroccan Air Force.

French citizens. The French decided they needed to discourage the Polisario from capturing French citizens. In December, Paris sent nine Jaguar aircraft, two KC-135 tankers, and a few support transports to Dakar, Senegal. The French also employed aerial reconnaissance to detect Polisario movements and base camps. Based on the combination of good intelligence and capable fighter aircraft, the French were soon able to make devastating attacks on Polisario columns. Within two weeks the Polisario returned its hostages to French authority. Even though the French quit attacking the Polisario, they kept their Jaguars in Dakar for several more weeks to assist the Moroccan air force in locating the Polisario but did not actually participate in any further attacks.[27] The success of the French attacks made the Polisario reluctant to operate in Mauritania. For a while the Front shifted its operations further north to the southern part of Morocco.

The French emphasis on using good intelligence and air power to achieve a specific political-military goal paralleled British air control policy. And, as in British air control, the psychological impact of an effective air control effort had an immediate and lasting impact on the enemy—the Polisario have not tried to pressure the French in any way since the 1977 incident. The effectiveness of French air power was a precursor of things to come as the Moroccan air force improved its capability in the period from mid-1979 through late 1981.

Incipient Offense (July 1979 to September 1981)

Between the summer of 1979 and the fall of 1981 the level of violence in this desert war increased, while Morocco stood alone against the Polisario and its Algerian and Libyan sponsors. During this period the capabilities of the Moroccan air force grew rapidly and Moroccan tactics improved quickly. It was also a time of important operational reforms in Morocco's conduct of the war in the south, reforms induced by Polisario successes in 1980.

The Polisario began to step up its attacks in January 1979 with its so-called Houari Boumediene offensive in honor of the Algerian president (who had died in December 1978).[28] The Polisario, freed from operations in Mauritania, had more resources to pit against the Moroccans and began to launch large-scale attacks against Moroccan positions in Western Sahara. Morocco's diplomatic efforts against the Polisario had fared badly in 1978–79, leaving Rabat no alternative but to increase its military offensiveness.

One of the first steps Morocco took to increase pressure in the south was to form Task Force Ohoud in August 1979. In three weeks this 6,000-man task force, under the command of Colonel-Major Ahmad Dlimi, swept from Benguerir in central Morocco to Dakhla, the capital city of what had been Mauritania's section of the Sahara.[29] The Polisario chose not to face off against the enormous firepower of this Moroccan column and the task force reached Dakhla with few incidents in November 1979. Task Force Ohoud discovered several Polisario supply caches and base camps but made little contact with the guerrillas. Although only modestly successful, the task force was a move, however tentative, away from the "hold the towns" mentality that had characterized previous Moroccan military efforts in the south.

During the fall of 1979, the Polisario mounted a major attack on Semara, a religious center of Western Sahara. The Polisario attacked with 2,000 to 5,000 men. The Moroccan garrison of 5,400 men held its own until a new factor could be brought to bear on the battle: Morocco's new Mirage F-1 fighters, which could operate day or night. Operating at night, the Mirages inflicted heavy damage on the Polisario, both on the units operating at Semara and on reinforcements coming across the desert.

Morocco's increased effort in the south, as reflected by Task Force Ohoud and the qualitative increase in air power resources exemplified in the presence of the Mirages, caused the Polisario to change its tactics in at least two ways. First, the Polisario reverted to small unit guerrilla tactics rather than large-scale attacks such as the one at Semara. Second, early in 1980 the Polisario began to increase its activities in Morocco proper. This effort may have backfired. The Moroccans were pushed into making significant military reforms as a result of the attacks within their boundaries, and the increased Polisario activity inside Morocco was an important argument used by the Carter administration to justify additional military support for Rabat.[30]

The Polisario's attack on Zag in southern Morocco was a major turning point in the war. The Moroccans formed a second task force, Zallaca, early in 1980 to clear the Polisario from the Ouarkziz mountains where the rebels had succeeded in isolating the town of Zag. Task Force Zallaca failed to dislodge the guerrillas and had to be reinforced by another task force, Al Arak. In May 1980 Morocco began a counteroffensive to relieve Zag. Although this relief effort eventually succeeded, Morocco's forces were, during the next several months, unable to dislodge the Polisario from Moroccan home territory. King Hassan and the senior Moroccan leadership viewed this situation as a humiliation to Morocco and its military forces. Hence, in the spring of 1980, Morocco's armed forces initiated significant reforms.[31]

Dlimi, now a brigadier general, was put in charge of all forces south of Agadir. Hassan, because of two previous military-led coup attempts, had been loath to put significant power beyond his personal grasp. However, the situation in the south was desperate enough to force this concession. New equipment and additional personnel were sent south. Additionally, the command and control of the air force was improved by relaxing control from Rabat. Since a 1972 coup attempt that had involved the F-5 squadron, the air force had been under direct control from Rabat. Therefore, launching aircraft in the south against guerrilla attacks had been unnecessarily time consuming. Communication between the army and air force also became more effective as staffs of the two services began to work together under the new, on-the-scene leadership of General Dlimi.

These reforms led to more effective Moroccan initiatives. By late 1980 the Moroccan military had reversed the perception that it was losing the war to the Polisario. The air force, now getting intelligence from the Army and using a C-130 for command and control and for surveillance, began a series of strikes that had a serious impact on the Polisario. These attacks not only led to a high attrition of the rebel forces but also denied them the ability to operate freely in the desert. The air force undertook extremely successful operations at Akka, Guelta Zemmour, Hausa, Messeid, and elsewhere between the summer of 1980 and the summer of 1981.

In these operations the Moroccan pilots operated at altitudes and at speeds that made the SA-7s and SA-9s, which had appeared in the Polisario's arsenal, ineffective. They flew a few high-speed, low-altitude missions to deliver French cluster bomb units and established good cooperation between the army and air force by using C-130s as communication platforms. Meanwhile, the Polisario had improved its antiaircraft capability not only with the SA-7 and SA-9, but it also with ZPU-23 antiaircraft artillery. And the Front had seemingly inexhaustible supplies of 122-mm rockets and ammunition for assaulting Moroccan fixed positions. Nevertheless, the Royal Moroccan Air Force had hurt the Polisario's ability to strike at will. This development limited the Polisario's heretofore unchallenged initiative.

By late 1980 Morocco was in the best position militarily that it had been in for a long time. The Moroccans realized, though, that they would never have the resources to control all of Western Sahara. So they decided on a strategically defensive move that fit in nicely with the defensive posture they had been in for most of the war. This step was destined to be one of immense importance; it sent important political and military messages to everyone concerned with this war.

Morocco's leaders in Rabat decided to build a barrier to protect the population and economic centers of Western Sahara. The barrier, called a *ceinture* or belt, would be primarily an earthen wall and would include fortified positions at various points, mine fields, and intermittent radar surveillance posts scattered along its perimeter (fig. 6 to 9). Anything of any value in the Sahara would be protected behind this wall: the major cities, virtually all of the population, the Bu-Craâ mines, and a large force of the Moroccan army. The army would hold strong points, have mobile reaction units, and have quick access to air power based at El Ayoun. Tactically the barrier presented a formidable problem for the Polisario. Once the ceinture was in place, the rebels would have to penetrate this defensive wall to be effective; if they penetrated at one point, they would be "walled in" and vulnerable to devastating counterattack. Politically the wall sent another message: the Moroccans are staying in Western Sahara regardless of the diplomatic and military pressures anyone may impose. Construction on the barrier began in the summer of 1980 and was completed in the summer of 1982. Eventually it followed a path nearly 750 kilometers long and enclosed all the "useful" area of the Sahara (fig. 10). The Polisario made dozens of raids during its construction but failed to stop the belt from being erected.

From the summer of 1980 to the fall of 1981, specifically to 13 October, the Polisario was on the defensive primarily because of the increased effectiveness of the Royal Moroccan Air Force. The Moroccans were using one C-130 for reconnaissance and command and control even though the aircraft had none of the sophisticated sensors one normally expects from today's tactical air reconnaissance platforms. In June 1980 the Moroccan air force made successful attacks on Polisario forces at Hausa, flying 10 Mirage F-1 sorties a day, a fairly impressive effort. In July the Mirages attacked Polisario "Stalin Organs," 40-tube banks of 122-mm rockets mounted on truck beds, at Messeid. Between late March and early April 1981 the air force experienced perhaps its most intense level of activity in conflicts around the Guelta Zemmour area. The Polisario attacked Guelta Zemmour in strength and drove out the Moroccan garrison. The air force covered the army's retreat, flew air cover for advancing reinforcements, and intercepted two Polisario battalions joining the fight in late March. The Moroccan air force inflicted considerable damage on the Polisario.

After Guelta Zemmour the Polisario clearly was on the defensive. The RMAF had effectively found and hit the Polisario, had developed tactics that negated the

Polisario SAMs, had improved air-ground coordination, and was beginning to integrate a nascent tactical air intelligence capability with its fighter forces. The Polisario had been so bloodied that the top leader of the Moroccan air force believed that it had effectively eliminated the Polisario as a military threat.[32] The Polisario did indeed reduce operations during the summer of 1981, but by the fall its forces were back, and with a vengeance.

SA-6 Induced Paralysis (October to December 1981)

A second major attack on Guelta Zemmour began on 13 October 1981 and lasted for 10 days. This attack was yet another turning point in the evolution of this long and indecisive war. The Polisario attacked the 2,600-man Moroccan garrison with about 3,000 troops. Besides the usual "Stalin Organs" the Polisario brought with them two new types of weapons: T-54 and T-55 tanks and SA-6 surface-to-air missiles.[33]

The SA-6 was the biggest surprise. It is an exceptionally capable and mobile surface-to-air missile, the same one the Israeli air force worked so hard to eliminate from Lebanon. This weapon system requires a high degree of training and maintenance skill to keep it operational. No one in Morocco dreamed that the Polisario had access to the SA-6, although the far less capable SA-7 and SA-9 had been on the battlefield for several years. Obviously the improved effectiveness of the Moroccan air force had driven the Polisario to obtain a weapon capable of countering the RMAF's F-5s and Mirage F-1s.

In this second battle of Guelta Zemmour, the Moroccan garrison was again driven out. The Moroccan air force lost two Mirage F-1s, its only C-130 command and control platform, and one F-5; in addition one Puma helicopter was damaged. The loss of two Mirage and one F-5 pilot was especially devastating to the Moroccan air force—it had lost only four Mirage pilots over the entire previous course of the war. The Moroccans retook Guelta Zemmour, but later abandoned it as they retrenched behind the belt.

The presence of the SA-6 in the Sahara had a paralyzing effect on the Moroccan air force. Although this paralysis eventually dissipated, as of July 1982 its effects had not entirely disappeared. The Moroccan pilots had no experience against a SAM as capable as the SA-6, and had no readily available information on how to cope with it. The air force's first reaction was to sharply reduce its flying beyond the belt. From October to mid-December 1981 practically no air force missions were flown against the Polisario. The failure of the air force to operate in the south provoked the ire of the army, which felt naked without air cover. The disaster at Guelta Zemmour also encouraged "finger pointing" between the army and air force on who was responsible for the defeat. The fragile working relationship slowly built up by the army and air force units in the south was shaken by the reluctance of the RMAF to operate against the SA-6.

Figures 6 and 7. A Portion of the Ceinture Near Bu-Craâ.

MOROCCO-POLISARIO WAR

Figures 8 and 9. Close-ups of Defensive Positions Along Ceinture.

THE AIR FORCE ROLE IN LOW-INTENSITY CONFLICT

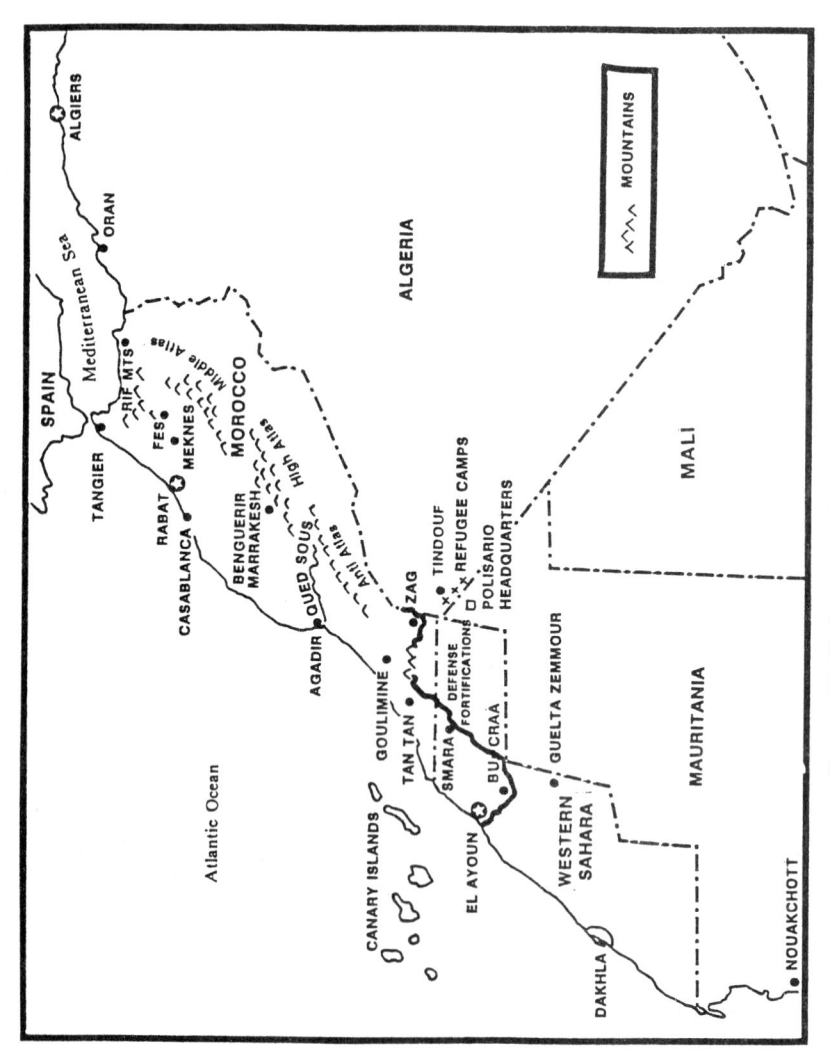

Figure 10. Reference Map: Saharan War.

The small number of T-54 and T-55 tanks (reports differ, but the number was certainly fewer than 10) that the Polisario used in the attack on Guelta Zemmour reinforces a notion suggested by the presence of the SA-6s. The Polisario, a ragtag group of perhaps 5,000-8,000 North Africans with no economic means of support except that provided by Algeria and Libya, has access to very sophisticated and quite heavy weapons. The picture of guerrilla warfare as a rebel force armed with automatic weapons is no longer a valid one. In the case of the Sahara war, the guerrillas can match or even surpass the firepower of their opponent. The impact of these heavy weapons on guerrilla tactics, and the possible vulnerability of massed heavy weapons to air power, remains to be seen.

Aftermath of Guelta Zemmour (January 1982 to Present)

The disaster at Guelta Zemmour drove the Moroccans in several directions simultaneously. First, the air force experimented with its Mirages, which have very basic electronic countermeasure equipment (such as radar warning receivers and chaff and flare dispensers), to "test" the SA-6. They very carefully tried to determine "safe" altitudes in which to operate with SA-6s present. This action was a limited one, fraught with danger; it did not yield conclusive results.[34] Second, during January 1982, the air force again went on the offensive, but in a very limited manner. Third, the Moroccans withdrew behind their defensive barrier and prepared themselves again for a long, defensive war. Finally, the Moroccans went to the United States for help.

In the Moroccan view, Washington recently had moved dramatically closer to Rabat. Ambassador Reed had long been saying that the United States was "with Morocco," and King Hassan was well aware of the US desire for basing options in Morocco in case of a Mideast contingency. Further, the Moroccans see their war with the Polisario as a fight against Soviet-supplied Communists intent on overthrowing the pro-West regime of King Hassan. The opinion was likely shared at the highest levels of the State Department in October 1981. With that sort of background, Hassan felt he could count on US assistance to solve the highly technical threat posed by the SA-6.

NOTES

CHAPTER 3

1. Martha Wenger, "Reagan Stakes Morocco in Sahara Struggle," *Merip Reports*, May 1982, 22.
2. John Mercer, *Spanish Sahara* (London: Allen and Unwin, 1976). Chapter 1 has the best description of the Spanish Sahara's topography available.
3. John Damis, *Conflict in Northwest Africa: The Western Sahara Dispute* (Stanford, Calif: Hoover Institution Press, 1983), 25-29.
4. Lewis B. Ware, *Decolonization and the Global Alliance in the Arab Maghrib: The Case of Spanish Sahara* (Maxwell AFB, Ala.: Air University Institute for Professional Development, 1975), 28.
5. John Waterbury, *The Commander of the Faithful* (New York: Columbia University Press, 1970), 74.
6. Jerome B. Weiner, "The Green March in Historical Perspective," the *Middle East Journal* 33, no. 1 (Winter 1979): 22.
7. V. Thompson and Richard Adloff, *The Western Saharans* (Totowa, New Jersey: Barnes and Noble Books, 1980), 172.
8. David L. Price, "Morocco and the Sahara: Conflict and Development," *Conflict Studies*, no. 88 (October 1977): 5-6.
9. *Le Monde*, 19 February 1976, 5.
10. Damis, *Conflict*, 40-41.
11. Ibid., 42.
12. Interview by author with senior Moroccan military officials in Rabat, 22 March 1982.
13. Ibid.
14. The *Manchester Guardian Weekley*, 5 March 1978, 12, and 17 March 1978, 12.
15. *Africa: An International Business Economic and Political Monthly* (London, April 1981): 44.
16. *Defense and Foreign Affairs Daily* 11, no. 24 (15 December 1982): 1-2.
17. Barbara Harrel-Bond, "The Struggle for the Western Sahara, Part II: Contemporary Politics," *American Universities Field Staff Reports*, no. 38, 1981, 6.
18. 1960 US-Moroccan Security Assistance Agreement.
19. Bernard Gwertzman, "U.S. Drops Sahara Issue in Arms Sales to Morocco," the *New York Times*, 26 March 1981, 27.
20. Ibid.
21. Pranay B. Gupte, "US Aide in Rabat Has Mixed Reviews," the *New York Times*, 18 April 1982, 23.
22. Damis, *Conflict*, 129.

23. Much of what follows, especially insofar as RMAF activity is concerned, is based on my trip to Morocco from 7-28 March 1982. I visited all major RMAF installations and had extensive interviews with senior, middle-level, and junior officers of the RMAF.

24. Damis, *Conflict,* 70–71.

25. Ibid., 84.

26. This information was provided by the RMAF.

27. Tony Hodges, *Historical Dictionary of Western Sahara* (Metuchen, N.J.: The Scarecrow Press, Inc., 1982), 151–52.

28. Ibid., xxxvi.

29. Ibid., 258.

30. Based on the prepared statement of Honorable Harold H. Saunders, assistant secretary of state for Near Eastern and South Asian affairs, to House Committee on Foreign Affairs, *Hearing before the Subcommittee on Africa,* 96th Cong., 1st sess., 4 December 1980, 8.

31. Hodges, *Historical Dictionary,* 363–64.

32. Statement made by Colonel-Major Mohammed Kabbej to General Lew Allen, 22 September 1981, Washington, D.C.

33. "Desert Victory—Or Was It A Mirage?", *The Economist* 281, no. 7208 (24–30 October 1981): 43; "International News,"; Reuters Ltd., 6 November 1981; Smith Hempstone, "High Stakes in Morocco's 'Forgotten War'," *Reader's Digest,* June 1982, 26.

34. Based on discussions with Mirage pilots at Sidi Slimane AB, Morocco, 23 March 1982.

CHAPTER 4

THE ROYAL MOROCCAN AIR FORCE AND UNITED STATES' ASSISTANCE

After the second battle for Guelta Zemmour, King Hassan asked the United States to help solve the problems of the SA-6. It was a request the United States could not refuse. As noted earlier, Ambassador Reed, from his first day there, had been very clear about our intent to assist the Moroccans. In addition, the Reagan administration had decided that the failure of the United States to support the Shah of Iran had soured the trust many third world friends had in the United States. Moreover, Morocco's location at the mouth of the Mediterranean was being recognized as an important geostrategic chokepoint. Also, King Hassan's ability as a moderate Arab leader to communicate with Arab leaders representing every shade along the moderate to radical political spectrum was becoming increasingly important to US diplomatic initiatives in the Mideast. Finally, the need for staging bases in North Africa for the Rapid Deployment Joint Task Force made access to Morocco's airfields important. The administration realized that Morocco had serious economic problems, and that Hassan's regime might not survive an economic crisis and a major defeat in the Sahara. Thus, the United States decided to assist the Moroccans in general and the Royal Moroccan Air Force (RMAF) in particular. However, providing this assistance in an effective way proved much more difficult than expected. One of the basic problems was that nobody in Washington truly understood the capabilities, limitations, problems, potential, and nature of the Royal Moroccan Air Force—the organization that faced the SA-6 threat most directly.

The Royal Moroccan Air Force in Moroccan Politics

The Royal Moroccan Air Force finds itself in a difficult position. It is continuously involved in fighting a nasty war (often with unreasonable, at least by our standards, controls from Rabat), but at the same time must transform itself into a first-class, modern air force that can support Moroccan interests throughout Africa in the years ahead. The mission of the RMAF is made difficult by the fact that it has evolved to its present level of preparedness and effectiveness under very trying conditions.

When Morocco attained independence from France in 1956, a small air arm was one of the early requirements of the armed forces. However, the Royal Moroccan Air Force was not created as a separate service until 1964. Since that time it has gradually grown in size and capability with help primarily from France and the United States. Although Morocco obtained some Soviet aircraft during the 1960s (for example, MiG-17s, MiG-15s, MiG-21s, and AN-12s), none of those aircraft are operational today. Moreover, that Soviet assistance did not extend to organizational and tactical experiences of a lasting nature.[1]

The key event affecting the growth of the Moroccan air force occurred on 16 August 1972 when the F-5 squadron apparently fell under the influence of General Mohammed Oufkir, the minister of defense and chief of staff of Morocco's military forces (Forces Armees Royales).[2] Oufkir was thought to be totally loyal to the King; he enjoyed the monarch's full confidence and was clearly second in power only to the King.

The August 1972 coup attempt saw six pilots from the F-5 squadron intercept the King's Boeing 727 and try to shoot it down. The pilot of the King's aircraft, Mohammed Kabbej, radioed to the attacking aircraft that the King was dead and that Kabbej was taking the damaged airliner down. The King had not been hit and Kabbej's quick thinking and superb airmanship in landing the badly damaged 727 were credited with saving the monarch's life. The pilots of the F-5 squadron were arrested; many of them "disappeared." When Oukfir's masterminding of the plot became apparent, he and his close associates were purged. As it turned out, Oukfir had engineered not only the August 1972 attempt, but also one in July of the previous year when a group of noncommissioned officer trainees attacked the royal seaside palace at Skhirat where a birthday party for Hassan was in progress. This attack was part of a wider coup d'état attempt that fizzled out rather quickly.

Following the 1972 coup attempt, King Hassan took strong steps that stripped the military, especially the air force, of much of its power. Hassan took over as his own minister of defense and chief of staff. Hassan showed his apparently well-founded distrust of the military by virtually disarming the ground forces and tightly controlling ammunition and all military operations. Kabbej, the King's pilot, became inspector of the air force, equivalent to the chief of staff of the US Air Force.

Even though the loss of many experienced F-5 pilots during this episode has had a negative impact on the Moroccan air force to this day, the appointment of Kabbej as its commander has had a positive impact. In fact, the RMAF was really reborn in 1972 under Kabbej's dynamic leadership.[3] At the time of the coup attempt, Kabbej was chief pilot of Royal Air Maroc, Morocco's national airline. He was more than a pilot who happened to gain the trust of the King, however. Kabbej had spent most of his working life in the air force. His long association with the air force gives Kabbej a great deal of legitimacy to serve as its commander. He joined the Royal Moroccan Air Arm in 1957 and served as its chief from 1960 until 1963 when he left active duty to fly with Royal Air Maroc. But he kept a reserve commission in the air force. Thus, because of his active duty and reserve service, Kabbej is not regarded in the air force as an upstart whose only claim to fame is service as the King's personal pilot. He is a superb pilot who has flown a wide range of aircraft (from MiGs to Mirages), is a supremely confident and intelligent man, and has a great deal of personal charisma. Finally, Kabbej is the single point of authority for everything dealing with the air force—an especially important fact when one realizes that no such person exists in the Moroccan army.[4] All of these facts combine to make Kabbej a most powerful individual in the Moroccan military.

In addition, Kabbej is more than a loyal royal retainer and a bureaucrat with a great deal of power. He is a man with considerable vision on how the Royal Moroccan Air Force should be built and he is in a position to build it according to his vision. The RMAF, as it exists today, shows Kabbej's foresight at work.

Building Up the Royal Moroccan Air Force

Morocco hopes to achieve two basic goals in the buildup of its air force: to fight a successful war against the Polisario in Western Sahara and to build a national force that can defend Morocco against air attack and can project its power throughout North Africa in pursuit of possible future Moroccan national objectives. Some of the current and projected programs of the RMAF clearly reflect the dual purpose of Morocco's approach to strengthening its air force.

Facilities

A look at the RMAF's operating bases and support facilities immediately draws attention to the existence both of room for expansion and of several highly advanced capabilities that are, at this time, only marginally used. These two facts suggest that the Moroccans are planning a force which can be greatly expanded in the future. For example the RMAF's command center at Salé, built by Westinghouse Corporation at a cost of about $240 million, is the hub of a very modern air defense system that blankets all of Morocco. Radar stations throughout the country feed into the Salé center where operators track air movements throughout the nation. All the equipment at the center is operated by Moroccans (but some Westinghouse technicians remain as advisors and troubleshooters). Interestingly, the RAMF has many women technicians in its ranks; many of the computer and scope operators are women, quite a rarity in Islamic countries. Although the women are limited in the level to which they can progress (there are only 10 female officers in the RMAF), they are getting advanced technical training and are working alongside men, important indicators of the progressive outlook of the RMAF.

The air defense center at Salé is a facility designed with the future in mind, not just to meeting today's operational needs. Presently, Morocco has no aircraft sitting strip alert, armed and prepared for an air defense mission. Thus, the center is a paradox. It is a very expensive and modern facility that is being used at much less than its full capability. Its dividends will only be paid in the future when the center becomes the operational keystone in an effective air defense system. Should international tensions increase in the meantime, however, aircraft would have to be assigned to that mission.

Moreover, Morocco's command and control network functions under definite limitations. For instance, the only time the command center could really operate as a command center would be if Kabbej or King Hassan were on the scene ready to conduct operations. Independent action by the officers routinely running the Salé facility is unlikely. Furthermore, the controllers at the center are prohibited from communicating directly with fighter bases—they speak only to airborne aircraft. This restriction undoubtedly reflects King Hassan's lingering fear of what an effective air defense system could accomplish if guided by a potential usurper. In the meantime, the Salé air defense center serves primarily as a training ground for young Moroccan computer operators and air defense specialists.

The concern of the RMAF for Morocco's technological future is also reflected at the Precision Measurement and Evaluation Laboratory (PMEL) at Kenitra. This facility consists of four laboratories, concentrating on direct current, alternating current, microwave, and physical dimension. They are modern and well organized and are used by civilian organizations as well as the RMAF. The air force allots eight years to train a PMEL technician. The laboratory is essentially a national technical asset—again one that is being underutilized at present, but it will become more important as the Royal Moroccan Air Force develops. Kenitra also houses a central, computerized inventory system for the air force. This system locates all the spare parts at all the bases of the RMAF. By today's standards, it is a modest, even primitive, system, but it is the first of its type in the Moroccan military. This system is a stepping-stone toward future development and shows the RMAF's commitment to technological growth.

The main operating bases for fighters at Meknes (F-5 unit) and Sidi Slimane (Mirage F-1 unit) also suggest commitment to the future. Both bases are well maintained; both have unused flightline and maintenance capacities. And Sidi Slimane has 24 hardened aircraft shelters that rival those of any air force in the world. The present threat and Morocco's current, limited air-to-air intercept capability hardly justify expending resources for hardened shelters. However, future requirements (which may include a need to project power on a regional level) will be well served by the ability to expand that is built into current RMAF facilities.

Training

These facilities would mean little without the qualified aircrews and support personnnel to make the air force an effective unit. The Moroccans are expending a great deal of their meager resources on building a first-rate training establishment. The heart of their officer training system is the air academy at Marrakech. The school opened eight years ago with only 14 students. In 1982 there were 120 students; the goal for 1983 is for 150 students. In 1982, there were 5,000 applicants for the 120 openings in the academy. Of those 120 students about one-half are expected to become pilots.

However, pilot production, especially for fighter pilots, is quite slow. Figures 11 and 12 show the time it takes to train a Mirage F-1 or an F-5 pilot and the small number who successfully qualify. The two and one-half years needed to become basically qualified in the Mirage and the three years for the F-5 are much too long by US standards. The shortage of fighter pilots is perhaps Morocco's greatest deficiency in its air war against the Polisario. But, because the time lag in training fighter pilots is so long, there is no quick fix for this problem.

The Force

In contrast, Morocco's air force does not seem to be short of aircraft. The Royal Moroccan Air Force has an interesting variety of aircraft in its inventory. Perhaps the area in which it is strongest is in support aircraft. The main contribution of the RMAF in the early phases of the war was aerial resupply done primarily by C-130H aircraft. Currently (as of 1983), the Moroccans have 15 C-130s with 35 pilots and copilots available—an adequate pilot to aircraft ratio. The RMAF maintains its C-130s at a 60-70 percent operationally ready rate, not bad considering that Morocco has horrendous problems getting spare parts for its aircraft. One of the C-130s is equipped with side-looking airborne radar (SLAR), which gives it an important surveillance capability as long as it does not get too close to surface-to-air missiles. Two additional SLAR kits are on order. In addition, Morocco has purchased two KC-130 airborne refueling aircraft and has recently obtained a Boeing 707 with a refueling pod. The air force inventory also includes several other transport aircraft. The Moroccans have two Mystere Falcon 20s and a Mystere Falcon 50; all three aircraft have some electronic countermeasures (jamming) and perhaps intelligence collection capability.

Morocco's training fleet consists largely of aircraft that were once strike aircraft. The most advanced trainer is the Alpha Jet. During 1982, the RMAF

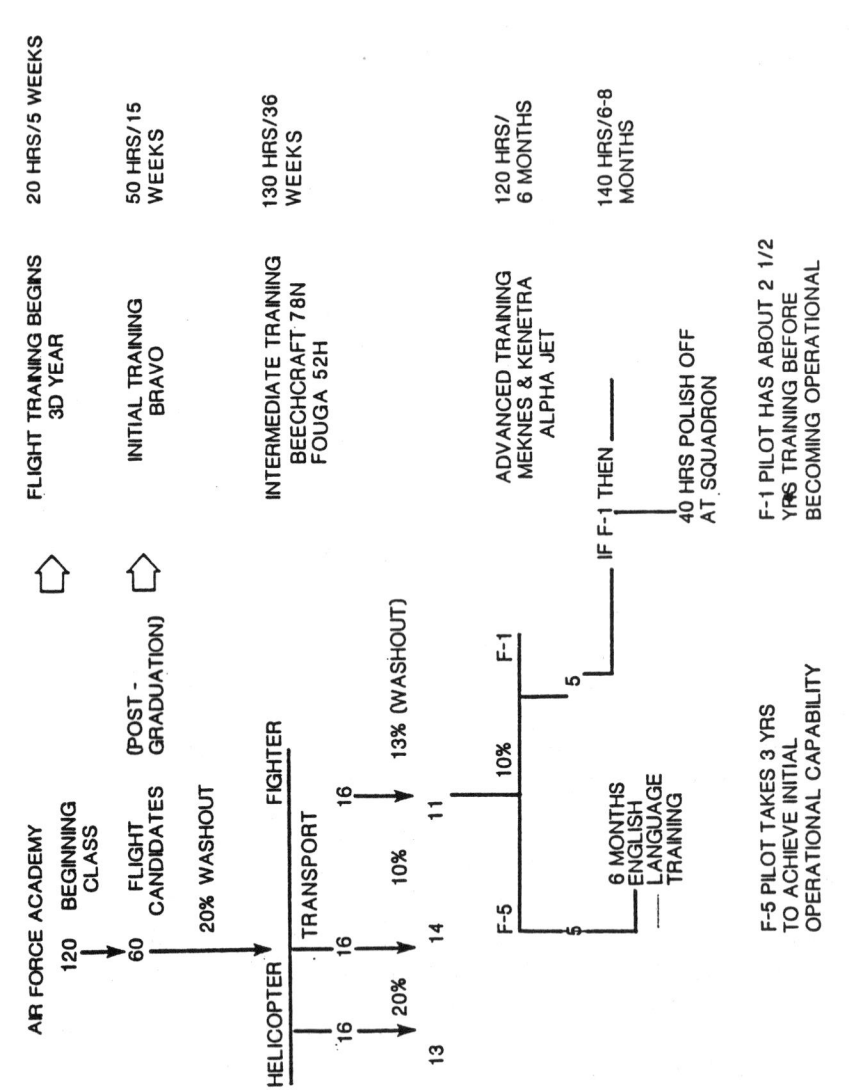

Figure 11. Pilot Production in 1982.

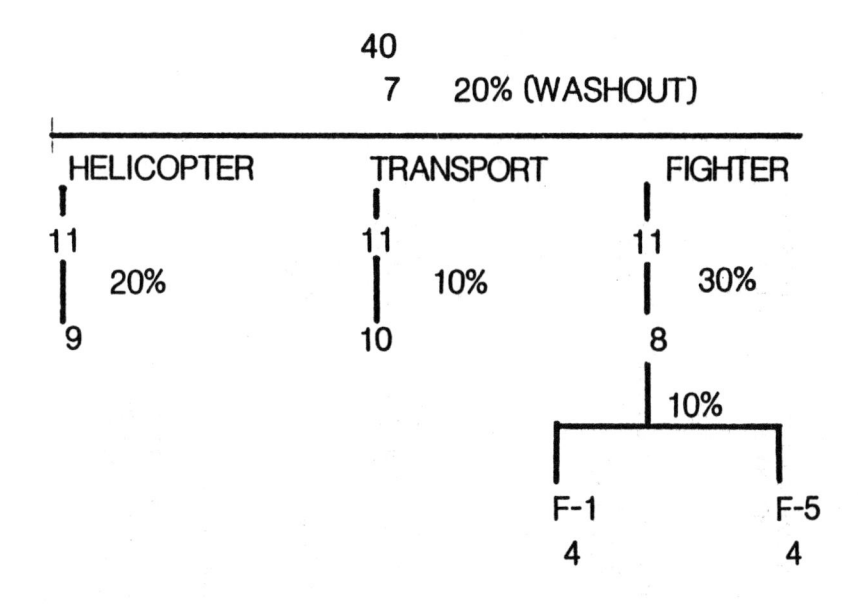

```
                    40
                    7    20% (WASHOUT)
────────────────────────────────────────────
  HELICOPTER        TRANSPORT        FIGHTER
  |                 |                |
  11                11               11
  |   20%           |   10%          |   30%
  9                 10               8
                                     |  10%
                                  ┌──┴──┐
                                  F-1   F-5
                                   4     4
```

Figure 12. Pilot Production in 1982.

used 24 of these aircraft for training; however, only 7 students and 4 French and 3 Moroccan instructor pilots took part in this flight training program. One squadron of Alpha Jet trainers, 12 aircraft will eventually go back to a ground-attack role. For initial training role, the Moroccan air force uses 9 AS-15 Bravo aircraft; for intermediate training, it utilizes 12 T-34 Mentors and 26 CM-170 Fouga Magister aircraft. Only between 40 to 50 pilots are being trained in the Mentor, Fouga, and Bravo programs.

The Moroccan air force has a sizeable fleet of helicopters, including 37 Agusta Bell 37s, 4 Agusta Bell 206s, 4 Agusta Bell 212s, 6 CH-47s, 21 SA-330 Pumas, and 6 SA-202 Gazelles. Eighteen more Gazelles are to be delivered under current contracts. The Gazelles will be equipped with antitank missiles. Morocco has enough helicopter pilots; they had done some creditable work in the war zone flying flank reconnaissance for moving ground forces.

Morocco also has six OV-10 aircraft. These planes were part of an arms deal with the United States that also brought over F-5Es. The Moroccan air force has only two pilots trained to fly the OV-10. However, these aircraft have never been used for combat missions. They are too slow and too vulnerable to SA-7 attacks to use in the war zone and are currently of little value to the RMAF. One possible role might be in sea patrol along the Moroccan-Saharan coast to protect Morocco's rich fishing grounds from encroachment.

The Moroccan fighter force has the potential to become an effective source of strength. It has been carrying the battle to the Polisario in recent years with its Mirages and F-5 Freedom Fighters. The RMAF has a sizeable number of French Mirage fighters; it has 24 F-1CHs and 15 of the more advanced F-1EHs. The F-1CH, which is equipped to carry manually released weapons, is used primarily in a ground-attack role; the newer F-1EH has more advanced radar and electronics and can carry automatically released ordnance. Morocco has 8 F-5A and B Freedom Fighters and 13 F-5E and F-5 Tiger IIs. Although there are 12 qualified F-5A and B pilots, these older model F-5s are all rarely used. In contrast, the RMAF has only 6 pilots qualified to fly the more advanced E and F models. Since the F-5s do not have radar warning receiver (RWR) gear, they are used only minimally in the war zone. Six more F-5Es with radar warning receivers are on order. These additional aircraft will place further demands on the already too few pilots qualified to fly this model of the F-5. Moreover, the F-5 unit is still suffering the aftereffects of the 1972 purge that followed the assassination attempt against Hassan II. Finally, the best F-5 pilots have been skimmed off to fly the more capable Mirages. The lack of qualified pilots rather than insufficient airframes is the main factor limiting an expanded Moroccan air war against the Polisario.

But when considering the current capability and potential of a third world air force such as the RMAF, one needs to differentiate clearly between the notions of qualified pilots and the quality of the pilots. Although Morocco suffers from a shortage of qualified pilots, they do not show a lack of quality. Becoming qualified is a function of effective training; we can judge the quality of pilots in terms of their loyalty, dedication to service, and capacity and willingness to learn. Based on these measures Morocco's pilots are quality officers. They are loyal to the King, anxious to help Morocco advance whenever possible, intelligent, and able. Senior RMAF officers are dedicated, professional, and loyal to the King. The line pilots and support officers respect their seniors and are a cohesive, capable group of men. Both the senior and junior officers interact well and debate problems openly and without rancor. It is a personal air force and one that fully understands its vital role in the Saharan war and its importance to Morocco's future. Judged on their performance, the RMAF pilots are clearly an elite group. With improved training programs, the personnel of the RMAF have the capability to make important strides to raise their skill levels. This point is an important factor to keep in mind while evaluating the air force's role and potential in the Saharan war.

Limitations of the RMAF

Good facilities and aircraft, quality people, and decent equipment and facilities provide a basis for developing a quality air force in the years ahead. The limitations on the RMAF today, however, far outweigh these positive attributes, a situation that is to be expected in an air force that is developing while simultaneously fighting a war.

Inadequate Training

The number one problem, fighter pilot production, has already been raised. The slow rate of training results in a gross imbalance in fighter asset-to-pilots ratio: 3 to 1 in the case of Mirages, slightly less for the F-5s. Basic F-5 pilot training is done in the United States, basic Mirage training in France. But these courses teach little more than rudimentary skills in handling the aircraft. Morocco also does not have a strong, effective program of advanced pilot training. Formation flying, air-to-air combat, ground attack tactics, and SAM tactics are done in the Moroccan units. Yet, because pilots and aircraft are so incredibly expensive for third world countries, these nations are loath to put either at risk. Hence, training is done as safely as possible, causing it to lack realism and intensity. The pilots rarely gain the confidence to take the aircraft to the limits of its performance capability. Thus, the expensive weapon systems that Morocco and other developing countries are buying in impressive quantities are rarely used to their potential.

Poor Army-Air Force Relationship

A second limitation on the effectiveness of the RMAF is the lack of adequate training with the ground forces and the failure to develop effective coordination of air-ground tactics. This situation, in part, stems from the competition between Colonel-Major Kabbej, the head of the air force, and senior army officers who compete for the King's attention and favor. That competition hampers effective staff work between the two organizations. Besides, King Hassan has purposely fragmented the army to limit its potential political power. Thus, the army does not have a chief of staff who can coordinate activity between the various branches of the ground forces. Rather, each branch operates autonomously— there is virtually as much difficulty in coordinating between army branches as between the army and the air force. This fragmentation of the army makes joint army-air force training quite difficult.

Further, the Moroccan air force and army differ in a fundamental way, a difference that is not uncommon in any nation's military. Morocco's air force is technologically much more advanced than its army. This is a fact brought on by necessity. The aircraft, simulators, communication equipment, weapons, and similar equipment that comprise an air force create a need for technological expertise. The Salé air defense center and the air force's computerized spare parts management system have no parallels in the army. In attitude and training, the air force is technologically a different animal than the army, and that makes communication between the two difficult.

In spite of these difficulties, some progress is being made in joint army-air force coordination and planning. The air force has trained 20 army men to act as ground controllers for air strikes. These troops are much like US ground-based forward air controllers and have been trained in air force communication techniques and weapon systems capabilities. For example, the RMAF has adapted from the French a manual on ground-air coordination. But, although the manual is available in the field, the extent of its use is not known.

The current practices at El Ayoun, the command air base in the war zone, provide the best evidence of this progress. The air commander at El Ayoun has a direct link to the ground-force communications net and is in constant contact with officers operating along the belt. They exchange information, analyze Polisario activity, and work together in planning and evaluating the effectiveness of air strikes. The working relationship between the army and the air force in the war zone is very good and stands in stark contrast to the situation in Rabat.

Inadequate Air Intelligence

A third serious weakness of the Royal Moroccan Air Force is the lack of adequate air intelligence. In 1981 the RMAF took the initial step in an effort to correct this deficiency when it created an intelligence section at the headquarters level. But this unit was allocated just one officer and no staff. With no formal training in air intelligence, this officer will be unable to make a noticeable contribution toward building an effective intelligence capability for quite some time. Meanwhile, the Moroccan air force is faced with several shortcomings in intelligence skills and intelligence equipment. It has only rudimentary film processing and readout equipment. And, although the SLAR-equipped C-130s provide the Moroccans with a good intelligence collection platform, the RMAF must recruit and train able people for intelligence work. It must also learn and adopt modern intelligence concepts and methods to use its equipment effectively. Additionally, the Moroccans must buy the right kind of equipment in the future, a step that will require developing considerable intelligence expertise within the service. Likewise, the Moroccans have not developed a systematic program for collecting, analyzing, and using intelligence. Nor have they learned the related concepts of targeting, selecting the best ordnance for destroying a given target, and assessing strikes. These support activities are essential if the air force is to use its assets fully.

Ineffective Planning

A fourth problem facing the Royal Moroccan Air Force is the lack of an effective planning staff. The Moroccans have established a planning section at their Rabat headquarters but have no one assigned to it. The planning is done by its top three leaders: Colonel-Major Kabbej, his deputy, and the director of operations. These men carry in their heads the needs and vision for developing this air force. Even though they are extraordinarily capable men, they do not have the time and energy to meet their demanding schedules and, at the same time, do an effective planning job.

In short, the major weakness of the Moroccan air force is its lack of midlevel staff officers to develop and conduct intelligence operations and joint training exercises, to do the planning necessary to ensure that the RMAF can perform its mission successfully, and to design the doctrinal basis for the air force. The demands of the war and the need "to put rubber on the ramp," when compared to the relative unimportance of support structures, make this situation understandable. But, if the RMAF is to develop fully over the next 20 years or so, it must begin now to develop the infrastructure that will enable it to become a potent force.

United States Assistance to the Royal Moroccan Air Force

The United States has long been involved with supporting Morocco's armed forces. In the past, this involvement has been quite limited; Washington was always a distant second to Paris in providing assistance to Rabat. However, over the last several years, the political and military importance of Morocco has grown considerably in the eyes of the United States. The result has been a significant increase in US defense assistance to Morocco.

The United States began supplying Morocco with arms in 1960. From 1960 through the late 1970s, this arms program concentrated on modernizing Morocco's overall military posture and did not relate specifically to the war in the south. For instance, after a 1974 visit to assess Rabat's defense needs, Brig Gen Edward Partrin (US Army) recommended equipping two Moroccan armored brigades stationed along the Algerian frontier. This equipment was to be provided through military sales (not aid) at a cost of about $500 million with delivery to be completed by 1980.[5] US military credits to Morocco from 1975 to 1980 ranged between $14 million and $45 million a year—far too small to finance major arms purchases.[6] Morocco had been receiving help from wealthier Arab states, especially Saudi Arabia, to buy arms for quite some time.

The situation changed in the late seventies. In 1977 Morocco asked for military assistance to cope specifically with the Polisario. The Moroccans requested OV-10 aircraft and attack helicopters. However, a 1960 security assistance agreement between the United States and Morocco stipulated that US-supplied weapons could be used only for internal security and self-defense. This particular agreement was designed to prevent American arms from being used against Israel. The Arms Export Control Act, which applies to all US foreign arms sales, similarly limits the use of US-supplied weapons. During congressional hearings in March 1978, the State Department said that the Moroccans had been using US-supplied F-5 aircraft in the Sahara but that their action was not a "substantial violation" of US law.[7] At the same time, Morocco's request for OV-10s and helicopters was shelved. The Carter administration was limiting arms sales to Morocco apparently because the Moroccans were using US arms in offensive actions in the Sahara. President Carter did allow Morocco to buy six CH-47C Chinook transport helicopters because these could be considered "defensive" weapons. The Carter administration's refusal to support Morocco was bitterly resented by the Moroccans who, to this day, have unpleasant memories of US policy in the Carter era.

In the summer of 1979, the Carter administration began to revise its position on support for Morocco. It used the successful Polisario attacks in Morocco proper to justify providing what had been considered as offensive arms, namely parts for F-5s being used in the south.[8] By the fall the Carter administration had completely reversed its position and approved a $235-million arms sale to Morocco, including 6 OV-10 armed reconnaissance aircraft, 20 F-5E fighters, and 24 Hughes helicopters—half of which were to be armed with antitank missiles, the other half with guns.[9] The administration was apparently reacting to a number of pressures besides the Polisario attack in southern Morocco. A need to show that the United States is reliable in support of its third world friends and a good deal of pressure from Saudi Arabia, which financed the deal, were major factors that affected the decision to allow Morocco to buy weapons that would be brought to bear against the Polisario in the Sahara.

Hearings in January 1980 by both the House Subcommittee on Internal Security and Scientific Affairs and the Subcommittee on Africa concerning the proposed aircraft sales to Morocco were heated.[10] On one side stood Congressman Stephan Solarz (D-NY). He believed the arms sales were not in US interests, would hurt US relations with Nigeria and Algeria, and would, in effect, suppress a genuine national liberation movement. In contrast, the Carter administration reiterated the need to support America's friends—a need made all the more poignant with the fall of the Shah of Iran, the need to offset Soviet arms available to the Polisario, and the need to bolster the Moroccans' confidence to encourage them to move toward a negotiated settlement. In the end, these two congressional committees tied the arms deal to progress in negotiations by Morocco. This proviso, obviously, was difficult to measure and implement.

Early in 1980, the United States had made an important shift in its attitude toward the Morocco-Polisario war. Assistant Secretary of State for Near Eastern and South Asian Affairs Harold H. Saunders testified that the administration had decided that "an outright military victory . . . by Morocco's adversaries would constitute a serious setback to major US interests in this area."[11] The Saharan war now had become a major US interest, whereas in the past the United States had been unwilling to support the Moroccans in their fight with the Polisario in Western Sahara.

The trend toward support of the Moroccans was vigorously pursued when the Reagan administration took office in January 1981. One of Secretary of State Alexander M. Haig's earliest initiatives was to support Morocco's request for 108 M-60A3 tanks with a price tag of $89 million, a request which had been shelved by the Carter administration. At the same time Haig rescinded the Carter administration's requirement that shipment of arms to Morocco would be tied to progress toward a negotiated settlement. This arms request ran into little congressional opposition.[12] Since then the Reagan team has continued a high level of support for Morocco. The Reagan budget for fiscal year 1983 raised foreign military sales credits to Morocco from $34 million to $100 million.[13] And Ambassador Reed, who maintained a high profile, started parading high-level Americans—Secretary Haig, Secretary Weinberger, Deputy Director of Central Intelligence Admiral Bobby Inman, Defense Intelligence Agency Director Lt Gen James Williams, and Senator Charles Percy, to name few—through Rabat.

The United States had been taking a very supportive stance toward Morocco for well over a year when the Guelta Zemmour disaster occurred in October of 1981. In light of these changes in the position of the United States, King Hassan probably felt that his request for help against the new, sophisticated SA-6 would not go unheeded. The appearance of the SA-6 in Morocco was a dramatic improvement in the forces of the Polisario and had a devastating impact on the ability of Morocco to continue achieving success on the battlefield. The Moroccans turned to the United States in the hope of immediate assistance.[14]

Meeting the SA-6 Threat

To meet the SA-6 threat the Moroccans needed help in several areas. First, to increase the proficiency of its aircrews, the RMAF needed specific training on how to operate in an SA-6 environment and how to attack that system. A critical factor for the RMAF was that its aircrews needed to know what the performance characteristics of the SA-6 were; whether it could be defeated by speed, maneuvering, or altitude; or whether a combination of flying tactics and appropriate electronic countermeasures (ECM) could defeat the SA-6. Yet, Moroccan pilots were not being instructed on how to fly in an SA-6 environment during the basic F-5 training they were getting in the United States. Thus, the first priority was to send US pilots to Morocco to provide this additional training. Second, the Moroccans also needed various kinds of ECM gear for their fighter aircraft. Their F-5s had neither radar warning receivers (RWR) to report when their aircraft had been acquired by radar nor chaff and flare dispensers. Although the Moroccan Mirage fighters had RWR gear, these aircraft did not have chaff and flare dispensers appropriate for dealing with SA-6s; they were set up for SA-7 and SA-8 missiles not the SA-6s. Finally, the Moroccans needed information: Where were the SA-6s? How many were there? What was the Polisario's refire capability?

The need to help the Moroccan air force meet the SA-6 threat pointed up some serious deficiencies in the ability of the United States and the US Air Force to help friends in the third world face difficult military challenges. The US Air Force had to overcome three problems in this effort. First, no one knew how proficient the Moroccan pilots were in basic flying skills. Second, the US Air Force had not developed a clear set of tactics for operating against the SA-6 other than the highly sophisticated Wild Weasel tactics—which were far beyond the capability of any third world air force. Third, the United States could provide training on only one of Morocco's two primary fighters, namely the F-5; yet the Mirage, the more capable of the two aircraft, was doing most of the fighting in the war zone.

The United States Air Force's response was to send a three-man training team to the F-5 unit at Meknes. Although the trainers did not know French, this language barrier was not as great an impediment as it could have been because the Moroccan pilots had learned a good deal of English as part of their F-5 training. The US pilots quickly found that the Moroccans had little capability in high-speed, low-altitude work—the very tactics the US team wanted to develop. The US team stayed in Morocco 60 days. Although the F-5 pilots improved their basic flying proficiency, primarily in formation and low-altitude flying, the US team concluded that Morocco's F-5 pilots would need much more training before they could go after SAMs—even if they did have improved electronic countermeasure equipment. Several Mirage pilots visited the F-5 unit to learn what they could from the Americans; however, the US pilots, who were unfamiliar with the Mirage, were of little help to Morocco's Mirage pilots.

The Americans favorably impressed the Moroccans with their skill in the aircraft, the intensity of their training program, and their ability and willingness to push the aircraft to its operational limit. Previously the Moroccans had been exposed primarily to the comparatively conservative and tame training programs of the French. The intense training philosophy of the Americans considerably impressed Morocco's pilots. For their part, the US pilots thought the Moroccans were excellent students, were willing to take risks, and had the potential to improve their flying skills greatly. Nevertheless, the US effort to train pilots to cope with SAMs did not accomplish its goal.

Our attempt to provide appropriate ECM equipment for the F-5s and Mirages also fell short. The United States thought it could provide immediate assistance by furnishing Morocco with 10 ALQ-119 ECM pods and 10 ALE-38 chaff and flare dispensers for the F-5s. (The best pod we have for the SA-6 threat, the ALQ-131, is not compatible with either the Mirage or the F-5.) The US offer was for a *nonrenewable* 180-day lease of the 10 ALQ-119s and ALE-38s with an installation and maintenance cost of $20 million to $40 million, payable in cash. The Moroccans—already strapped by a tough economic year, a drought, and the enormous cost of the war—did not have the cash to pay for the installation. Furthermore, a nonrenewable 180-day loan of equipment did not seem like a reasonable bargain. Instead Morocco shopped around and bought some ECM pods from the Italians and installed them on the Mirages. As a result, US credibility for supplying the right equipment at the right time suffered greatly.

Additionally, the United States had the capability to provide important intelligence to the Moroccans about the SA-6. Because of very high-level interest in helping the Moroccans, the United States made a concerted effort to locate the position of SA-6s operated by the Polisario. At considerable expense, US forces obtained specific intelligence data that could have been put to operational use by the RMAF. But, the United States did not develop clear procedures to transfer the intelligence that its personnel had gathered and analyzed to the people who could use the intelligence—the RMAF strike pilots at El Ayoun. On the one hand, the US intelligence community insisted on keeping the intelligence under tight control at a high level. On the other, Morocco did not use efficient procedures to disseminate the information properly from Rabat. Frequently the timely intelligence obtained by the United States did not reach the south in time to do any good.

The United States offered help to the Moroccans in yet another area. In November 1981, Assistant Secretary of Defense for International Security Affairs Francis J. West led a US delegation to review Morocco's security needs. He urged the Moroccans to engage in more aggressive, mobile counterinsurgency tactics. To that end he offered a team of 20 US ground force experts to train the Moroccans in commando-style tactics. One aim was to develop a special unit that could make commando-type attacks on SA-6 units in the desert, perhaps using helicopters. The US Army team sent to work with the Moroccans had no tested plan for coping with the SA-6 in a desert, so they invented tactics along the way. The Army team was working with an elite Moroccan battalion assigned to protect the King; it was, perhaps, the best equipped and trained unit in the Moroccan army. The effects of the US Army's training are yet to be seen. One hopeful sign is that a senior RMAF officer is now working with the Moroccan army to develop this special unit. The use of tactics involving ground forces, air cavalry, and fighter aircraft working together against the SA-6 might prove very interesting and successful. However, the US Air Force does not have any practical experience in developing those kinds of tactics for the use in the third world by third world air forces, so we can offer our friends little help in that area.

The one positive step that resulted from this short-term effort was that the United States finally decided to supply the RMAF with the cluster bomb units (CBU) it had been requesting for several years. These weapons are particularly effective against personnel, unarmored vehicles, and radar. The United States had refrained from allowing the Moroccans to buy cluster bombs because of their lethality. (The same policy applied to napalm.) But, we were now ready to sell the cluster bomb to the Moroccans to meet the SA-6 threat.

However, given its deficiencies as described throughout this chapter, the Royal Moroccan Air Force has used these expensive cluster bombs in a most profligate way. For example, in March 1982, five months after the Guelta Zemmour debacle, a flight of three Mirages and two F-5s operating from El Ayoun used these bombs to attack an area of suspected Polisario activity near the Bu-Craâ area. The planning for the operation was simple: reports from the army on Polisario activity were plotted on a map and an area perhaps 2 kilometers by 1 kilometer was sketched around the map points. The aircraft flew to predetermined coordinates, about a mile from the strike area, and "tossed" their bombs from the predetermined coordinates using the inertial navigation system of the Mirages. There was no pre- or poststrike reconnaissance of the target area, hence the results of the attack were not known. At best, it could have harrassed the Polisario; most likely it had no impact at all. This attack was a waste of the equipment at the disposal of the Moroccan air force. It shows too clearly the all-consuming caution the RMAF feels it must exercise where there is even the possibility of an SA-6 attack.

In spite of these US attempts to help the Moroccans neutralize the SA-6s, the missiles remained in the desert unharmed. Clearly problems existed on both the American and Moroccan sides. The United States had problems understanding the capability of the RMAF, imposed impossible limitations on providing ECM equipment, and failed to understand the workings of Moroccan politics. This situation yielded marginal returns. The Moroccan air force lacked basic capabilities in flying skills, had inadequate means to use intelligence, and had poor equipment—a combination that made a link up between what the United States could provide and what the Moroccans would use impossible. This experience raises several important issues: Should US Air Force improve its capabilities to assist a friendly third world air force? If small scale intervention is required, can the United States act effectively? Should there be organizational changes in the US Air Force to make an improved assistance and intervention role feasible?

NOTES

CHAPTER 4

1. Harold D. Nelson, ed., *Morocco—A Country Study*, 4th ed. (Washington, D.C.: The American University, 1978), 289–92.

2. The details of this coup attempt have never been made public. Harold Nelson's *Morocco—A Country Study*, referenced above, has the basic facts of the event on pages 78–79. The information contained in my paragraphs on the subject was gleaned from conversations with several mid- and high-level Moroccan officers in March 1982.

3. The information on Kabbej's background and on the organization, capabilities, limitations, and potential of the Royal Moroccan Air Force that follows is based on data gathered by the author while touring all operational RMAF bases during March 1982.

4. The Moroccan army, ten times the size of the RMAF, is potentially far too potent for the King to allow it to become too efficient. Thus, the army is kept decentralized and essentially leaderless.

5. John Damis, *Conflict in Northwest Africa: The Western Sahara Dispute* (Stanford, Calif.: Hoover Institution Press, 1983), 25.

6. Ibid., 26.

7. House Committee on International Relations, Subcommittee on Africa, *Hearings, Foreign Assistance Legislation for Fiscal Year 1979* (Part 3), 96th Cong., 2d sess., 159.

8. House Committee on Foreign Affairs, Subcommittee on Africa and International Organizations, *Hearings, US Policy and the Conflict in the Sahara*, 97th Cong., 1st sess., 23–24 July 1979, 14–15.

9. David H. Price, "Conflict in the Maghreb: The Western Sahara," *Conflict Studies*, no. 127 (February 1981): 10.

10. House Committee on Foreign Affairs, Subcommittees on International Security and Scientific Affairs and on Africa, *Hearings, Proposed Arms Sale to Morocco*, 96th Cong., 2d sess., 24–29 June 1980.

11. Ibid., 3.

12. Bernard Gwertzman, "US Drops Sahara Issue in Arms Sales to Morocco," *New York Times*, 26 March 1981, 24.

13. Martha Wenger, "Reagan Stakes Morocco in Sahara Struggle," *Merip Reports*, May 1982, 24.

14. The analysis of US attempts to help the Moroccans with the SA-6 problem is based on discussions held with Moroccan and American military and diplomatic personnel in Rabat and Washington, March–April 1982. Few public sources on this episode have emerged. The most complete such article is Tony Hodges, "The Endless War," in *Africa Report*, July–August 1982. Hodges' article, however, contains several significant errors of fact. Its bias toward the Polisario is also evident.

CHAPTER 5

MILITARY REQUIREMENTS FOR LOW-INTENSITY CONFLICTS: LESSONS FROM MOROCCO

The Moroccan experience in fighting a protracted guerrilla war and in seeking assistance from a professed, superpower friend has lessons at many political, diplomatic, and military levels. The attempt by the United States government to assist Morocco at a critical point in its war against the Polisario suggests several points about modern low-intensity conflicts, the role of the US military in general and the US Air Force specifically in such conflicts, and the requirements that would be generated by such involvements.

The overarching point is that low-intensity conflicts will not go away. There will be times when the United States must act to protect its interests and those of its friends, and when exercising specialized military capabilities will likely become a necessary and useful option to have as policymakers design a plan of action. The Morocco-Polisario war has been dragging on in spite of major diplomatic efforts by the King of Morocco, the United States, the Organization of African Unity, the United Nations, Saudi Arabia, and others. Most commentators believe that the conflict has no military solution, yet continuously escalating military activity seems to be a constant in the war. Until recently the United States was relatively uninvolved and unconcerned. During the first years of the Carter administration, US aid to Morocco was very limited. Only when Morocco's geostrategic position became a factor in US planning for Middle East contingencies did US aid to Morocco increase. After the Reagan administration assumed power, US policy closely embraced Morocco, promising strong support, even if that support was not clearly defined. Morocco's call for help came quickly. The United States government wanted to help, but failed to achieve the desired results.

Imprecise US Policies and Objectives

This failure occurred for many reasons. At the policy level, deciding to act on Morocco's behalf was hampered both by the complex international interests intertwined in this seemingly remote and inconsequential war and by the considerable internal squabbling within policy-making circles in the United States. On the one hand, the United States interest in maintaining Hassan in power as a pro-Western, moderate Arab leader in a country whose location is important to US strategies in the Mideast and on the southern flank of NATO. On the other hand, a less obvious but equally significant factor for US decision makers was the need, especially in late 1981 when the SA-6 crisis occurred, to deal fairly with Algeria, Morocco's real protagonist in the war. A strong faction in the US State Department believes that Algeria, not Morocco, will be the future leader of the Maghreb and that US interests would be better served by strengthening its ties with Algeria rather than Morocco. Moreover, many US policymakers would like to maintain access to Algeria's oil should other supplies be endangered. Finally, a desire to repay Algeria for its assistance in securing the release of US hostages in Iran also affected US planning to support Morocco in late 1981.

Another factor, which helps complicate the picture, is the high level of support provided to Morocco by Saudi Arabia. Saudi Arabia is now central to United States policy in the Middle East. Riyadh has played an important role as financial backer to many US allies and friends and is, in large part, financing Morocco's war against the Polisario. Saudi Arabia has a great deal of influence in Washington and its strong support of King Hassan must be considered as the United States formulates its Moroccan policy. Thus, many argue that we must back Morocco, even at the risk of antagonizing Algeria.

Arms control philosophy also had an important impact at the policy level. As discussed earlier, the US Congress had bitterly debated providing arms to Morocco for use against the Polisario. The legitimacy of Moroccan claims to Western Sahara had been deeply questioned in Congress and no clear consensus had been established defining US interests and responsibilities in the conflict. The crisis precipitated by the Polisario's SA-6 attack on Moroccan aircraft could only exacerbate concern about escalating US support to the Moroccans because dealing with the SA-6 would have to include considering such options as direct US attacks on the SA-6s or, much more likely, providing the Moroccans with the intelligence, electronic countermeasures, munitions, and training that would enable them to meet the threat on their own. The idea of direct action against the SA-6s was probably never considered as a serious option for US assistance. Our efforts concentrated on helping the Moroccans deal with the SA-6 themselves.

This effort revealed some institutional weaknesses in the Air Force and US security assistance programs. The three-man Air Force team sent to Morocco on

60-day temporary duty was able to work only with Morocco's F-5 pilots. These pilots were the least experienced pilots in the RMAF and flew an aircraft that is clearly a second stringer behind the Mirage F-1. The US pilots chosen to help the Moroccans had many handicaps going into the problem. They were professional flight instructors from the Air Training Command and had no special training in dealing with a third world air force, no training in understanding the Morocco-Polisario war, no ability to speak or understand French or Arabic, and no understanding of the flying proficiency of the Moroccan F-5 squadron.

Before the United States could aid Morocco effectively, those people in the Air Force and elsewhere who were responsible for developing viable assistance options had to understand fully the capabilities and limitations of the Royal Moroccan Air Force, the nature of the war the Moroccans were pursuing in the Sahara, and the impact of Moroccan politics on any military activity undertaken by the Moroccan armed forces. However, in proposing to help a third world air force meet a threat such as the SA-6, US military personnel often tend to analyze the situation in terms of their own experiences. In Morocco this tendency was evident. The plan developed to help the Moroccans applied the typical US Air Force solution of combining specialized tactical flying training with appropriate electronic countermeasure equipment; the Moroccans then would be able to attack the SA-6 themselves. If we added assistance in locating the target, it would make the Moroccans' task that much easier. But because our information on the Royal Moroccan Air Force was so limited and because we had only a marginal understanding of political-military relations in Morocco, our attempts at helping were ineffectual.

Moreover, the United States has great difficulty supplying sophisticated electronics equipment to a friendly third world country for political and practical reasons. Politically, many officials are reluctant to provide sophisticated equipment because of the fear of compromising US technological secrets. Additionally, many political decision makers resist any attempt to provide military assistance to a threatened friend because such assistance suggests an escalation in terms of the quality and sophistication of the arms involved in the conflict. From a practical standpoint, getting equipment that could be adapted to Morocco's first-line Mirage fighters proved infeasible; adapting the equipment to the F-5 was possible but impractical, primarily because of the terms we imposed on providing the equipment. A nonrenewable 180-day lease for equipment that cost many millions of dollars to install is not a very palatable offer for a country short of money and concerned with permanent improvements to its forces. In addition, this equipment, even if it could be provided permanently to Morocco, could be used only on the F-5, clearly Morocco's second-string fighter. If the US could have provided electronic countermeasure equipment for the Mirage that would have met the SA-6 threat, then perhaps our assistance could have been more productive. Certainly the flying skills of the Mirage pilots were much more advanced than those of the F-5 pilots. Our training assistance would have been much more beneficial had we been able to work with the Mirage unit.

Basic Requirements for Assisting a Third World Air Force

Effective assistance by the US Air Force to third world air forces in the future will require a major effort in at least three areas. First, the Air Force must acquire a much deeper knowledge of third world countries in general and third world military forces in particular. This effort requires that we give higher priorities to collecting and analyzing intelligence on most third world countries. Intelligence analysts and security assistance program managers normally tend to concentrate their efforts on the high-visibility, high-priority programs such as those in Israel, Egypt, Lebanon, and similar hotspots. Analysts covering less important areas normally have several countries to cover simultaneously. This division of responsibility precludes those analysts from building a really thorough knowledge about these smaller countries. Thus, when a crisis occurs, US policy formulators have inadequate information and are ill prepared to offer meaningful and effective options to assist a threatened friend. As seen in Morocco, a poor understanding of the capabilities of the Royal Moroccan Air Force resulted in ineffectual attempts to assist—the training and the electronic countermeasures the United States tried to supply failed to deal effectively with the problem at hand.

Second, the Moroccan experience points up the need for the United States and the Air Force to be able to transfer knowledge and techniques if they are to aid a third world country effectively and its air force. But our ability to transfer knowledge and techniques presupposes that we will have appropriate knowledge about third world countries and their military services, and will know what techniques and knowledge would be valuable for their air forces to acquire. It may not be appropriate, for example, to train a third world air force in the sophisticated aircraft and tactics used at the US Air Force's Red Flag facility at Nellis Air Force Base. Moreover, in terms of both flying skills and infrastructure, the US Air Force must identify those areas in which it is most qualified to provide assistance. Infrastructure includes the support elements that enable combat aircraft units to be viable components of an armed force—the planning, intelligence, logistics, and doctrinal organizations that make air power a powerful force. The Air Force must create training and infrastructure packages appropriate to developing air power in third world countries, not just to building smaller mirror images of the US Air Force. In short, we in the Air Force will have to exert the effort to identify a friendly country's weaknesses and be flexible enough to adapt our equipment and capability to respond to the host country's needs.

Once these kinds of training packages are built, techniques for transferring that knowledge effectively must also be developed. That means having the organization and the people to support work in third world countries. At present, the Air Force tends to attempt to transfer knowledge to third world militaries only in an ad hoc manner. (Transferring equipment is institutionalized within the Department of Defense military assistance programs.) The normal procedure is to wait for a foreign nation to request specialized training, usually in response to an immediate need, such as the SA-6 crisis in Morocco. The Air Force searches out those personnel who seem able to fill the requirement, pulls them from their current assignment, and sends them on temporary duty (TDY) to the problem area. Sometimes the TDY personnel get briefed on the political-military situation they will encounter, sometimes not. Language training usually cannot be provided to meet a short-term contingency. Thus, if knowledge of the language is mandatory, the selection of personnel is limited; and of course, the effectiveness of personnel who have no language capability will be limited since they must work through interpreters.

A related issue is the cross-cultural awareness of each member of the training team. Working with foreign nationals, especially the extremely proud elites of the developing world, is greatly eased if the US personnel are trained in the cultural mores of the country to which they are assigned. Yet, there are very few ways for an Air Force officer to become attuned to the subtleties of the cultures in which he may be required to work. The handful of officers trained as foreign area specialists is mostly concentrated in the intelligence, international political-military affairs, and office of special investigations career fields—career specialties that are not normally involved in transferring knowledge to allied or friendly countries. Some personnel sent abroad have the opportunity to participate in a USAF Special Operations School course on cross-cultural relations. However, it is very broad brush, and, thus, useful but by no means comprehensive preparation for entering a foreign culture as a teacher of complex ideas and equipment.

Third, the United States and the Air Force must develop the capability to react speedily to assist threatened third world friends. Being able to put the right combination of people and equipment on the scene fast would greatly impress third world friends and allies. The ability to act quickly depends on our first acquiring a knowledge of potential host countries and their militaries, and then building effective means to develop and transfer military knowledge and techniques to host countries. For a few countries such as Israel and Egypt, the United States has the knowledge and the capability needed to act with speed if the need arises; for most other countries, the US government has not applied the resources necessary to establish the base that makes quick and effective action possible.

Levels of Potential Air Force Participation

To be effective in low-intensity conflict, the Air Force and the United States must be flexible enough to act at three levels: assistance, integration of forces, and intervention. The Air Force can make an important contribution at each of these levels, both as an independent entity working directly with a third world air force and as a member of a joint service or joint agency effort.

Participation by the Air Force at the assistance level means working with third world air forces on both a short- and long-term basis. The Air Force can make its most important contribution to supporting US interests in the third world at this level of activity. This mission, called foreign internal defense, includes nation-building in conjunction with other US and host government agencies, assisting in training and equipping host country air units, and providing continuous guidance to indigenous air force units on employing equipment and techniques in military operations.[1]

The potential benefits of developing close training and working relationships on an air force to air force basis between the US Air Force and friendly third world air forces are many. Working with foreign air forces enables the US Air Force to gain tremendous insight into the capabilities, limitations, and potential of those air forces. This arrangement provides the essential knowledge needed to establish meaningful assistance programs that result in the appropriate growth of the host nation's air arm. Additionally, by working in an environment that could become a low-intensity battlefield at some point, the Air Force personnel involved in the training would gain knowledge invaluable should the United States need to intervene. Developing true interrelationships between the US Air Force and other air forces has the potential of increasing the political stability of a region and increasing US access to the region, and could even result in gaining a US proxy there. Those kinds of results, however, require long-term US Air Force to host nation air force programs, well-trained US Air Force people dedicated to developing close working relationships with other nations, conscious planning by the US Air Force that determines which countries of the world will be strategically important to United States foreign policy, and active seeking of air force to air force relationships in those countries. These kinds of foreign internal defense efforts are handled under two broad programs—military assistance and advisory groups (MAAGs) and mobile training teams (MTTs)—neither of which is currently effective.

Shortcomings of Assistance Programs

Our military assistance and advisory groups operate worldwide. (MAAGs, for our purposes, include all activities designated as military advisory groups, security assistance offices, offices of military or defense cooperation, and like agencies or activities; defense attachés are not part of the MAAG system.) However, in the aftermath of Vietnam, many US policymakers felt that the MAAGs were to blame for much of the failure of US policy in Vietnam and had no further role to play in US foreign policy.[2] Thus, the level of assistance offered through these programs was severely reduced. The Arms Export Control Act of 1976 was a major result of the debate on the US military presence abroad. This act set the tone for US policy in the middle to late 1970s regarding MAAGs; the number of MAAGs and the number of people involved in security assistance overseas were reduced significantly. The cutback in people led to reduced contact with host military offices, which generally eroded the ability of the United States to advise a host nation on the suitability of specific systems.[3]

This trend continued with the International Security Assistance Act of 1977 (Public Law 95-92). That law circumscribed MAAG operations and established a ceiling on MAAG manpower. Equally important, it established four areas that were to be the focus of MAAG activities: logistics management, transportation, fiscal management, and contract administration of country programs. Thus, the MAAGs were not responsible for providing host nations with help on long-range planning objectives, force development, strategy and doctrine development, or building the support infrastructure that makes military forces—especially air forces—useful parts of a defense establishment. The role of the MAAGs was changed from providing advice and assistance, as the name of the organization implied, to administering equipment contracts, collecting payments, and moving paper. MAAGs, therefore, have tended, for the past decade, to operate in capital cities and have had minimal contact with forces in the field. This condition exists for all the services represented in a MAAG, including the Air Force.

Contact with the field forces of nations the United States wishes to help has been primarily through mobile training teams (MTTs). These teams consist of military personnel with the specific skills needed by the host country. They make short-term visits (usually 30-90 days) to the host country. The teams are manned by representatives from each service, or more likely, from a single service. As noted in the Moroccan SA-6 crisis, the United States sent two teams: an Air Force team to teach flying skills and an Army team to teach ground tactics. The Department of Defense runs the mobile training teams through various foreign military assistance programs, but each service has its own way of selecting, supporting, and training the team members. The team sent to Morocco to solve the SA-6 problem is typical of the Air Force approach: an ad hoc team is selected and sent to do a complex job with little or no specialized training in the country or situation into which it is being thrust.

Despite of the lack of training for Air Force mobile training team members, the teams normally do a very creditable job, primarily because of the quality of Air Force people sent, the understanding by foreign nationals of our deficiencies in foreign language skills, and the eagerness of foreigners to learn from US personnel. The system could, however, be much improved. The specific organizational and personnel requirements to improve the effectiveness of US Air Force mobile training teams are discussed in chapter 7, but, as a minimum, the teams need a corps of expertise on regional areas that can provide in-country language and cultural assistance to MTTs.[4]

Problems of Integrating Forces

Assisting third world air force through the mechanisms of military training teams and in-country advisory groups may be inadequate in some instances. A friendly country may face an active internal or external threat requiring assistance beyond what assistance groups and mobile training teams, can provide, since they are not eligible to participate in combat. United States forces may need to integrate with indigenous forces to provide training *in combat*. The special problems of integrating US forces with host forces in a combat situation need special consideration by Air Force planners.

Integrating small contingents with host nation forces operating in the field would generate significant equipment and personnel requirements for the US Air Force. The Air Force has had no extensive experience with integrating special forces with host nations since the 1960s, when Air Force units operated with the Vietnamese and Laotians. The purpose of integrating small, specialized Air Force units today with host nation forces would be to provide training under combat conditions, to stiffen inexperienced local forces, to gain knowledge of local conditions for future Air Force planning, to test equipment and tactics in the field, and to provide a low-cost, low-visibility US presence in an area where such a presence is desired for policy reasons. Such a presence would require specially trained and equipped air forces—ones that could operate independently in cooperation with local forces, that are self-contained in communications, and that have minimal logistic and administrative overhead. The personnel operating in these kinds of situations would also need language and cultural training appropriate to the area as well as knowledge of local political and military institutions. Ideally, they would have equipment that could be supported by the host country. The most of the third world, where the need for US forces to train and stiffen host country forces is most likely, the Air Force capability to do so is nonexistent. Deploying primary Air Force general purpose forces—F-15, F-16, or A-10 units—in such situations is unrealistic. Those forces are trained almost exclusively to operate in European and Korean conflict scenarios. And they require very extensive and intensive logistic support and are not easily supportable in small elements. The equipment and techniques needed to support the front-line aircraft of the US Air Force cannot be readily adapted to provide the equipment and techniques needed to support the main fighter aircraft of the third world—F5s, various types of Mirages, and many other aircraft smaller and simpler than the front-line fighters of the United States.

In addition, the US Air Force special operations force—the one we would expect to work most closely with third world air forces—has become very narrow in its area of potential operations. It has no strike aircraft other than the AC-130 Spectre gunship, which must fly in a totally permissive operating environment. Other than the Spectre, the Air Force special operations force currently operates only the MC-130 Combat Talon, HH-53 Pave Low, and UH-1N helicopter. These aircraft are designed for a very narrow mission within the low-intensity conflict spectrum. In conjunction with other service forces, they can be used for direct action raids against specific targets, especially to insert and extract special action teams into and out of their area of operations. But these crews and aircraft are not appropriate for integrating with and augmenting a host nation's air force. Thus, a potentially significant option for a US decision maker wishing to assist a third world country is lost.

Limits to US Ability to Intervene

The Air Force also needs to assess its ability to act at another, higher level of low-intensity conflict: intervening unilaterally or in concert with allies in third world conflicts. The airlift capability of the US Air Force leaps to mind as one way in which it can act in intervention scenarios; so too does the capacity of the Strategic Air Command's strategic projection force (SPF) to deliver conventional bombs. The value of airlift to support the intervention forces of either the United States or others cannot be overstated. It is one area where air power is a visible and useful instrument of US power. The strategic projection force is both a visible and an important psychological element of US military force. The 35 B-52Hs assigned to the SPF have tremendous range and payload capabilities. The SPF also includes reconnaissance, intelligence, air refueling, and force management assets—KC-135A and Q, SR-71, U-2, RC-135, E-3A, and EC-135 aircraft. The heart of this force, though, is the B-52Hs, which have a range of about 8,800 miles and have been modified to carry 500-pound general purpose bombs, the same types of bombs dropped by B-17s in World War II.

However, despite the military power embodied in the SPF, its value as an employable element of US military force is severely limited. The destructive power of its bombs is poor, and their use suggests "carpet bombing" techniques rather than the precise application of firepower—yet precision, as shown in the British air control case, is a key to intervening successfully in small wars. Further, because they are gravity bombs (as opposed to long-range standoff missiles), they require overflight of the target. The availability of sophisticated SAMs to virtually any potential adversary makes overflight by B-52s using conventional tactics unattractive.[5] In addition, conventional bombing by B-52s would be a highly visible form of intervention in a low-intensity conflict, which given the currently available weapons, would be an imprecise application of firepower that could have negative psychological results. Nevertheless, inadequate as it may be in many respects, the strategic projection force is the only effective means the US Air Force has of applying firepower in the third world areas.

Under current operating concepts, Air Force tactical fighters have little or no role to play in low-intensity conflicts. The current fighters (F-15, F-16, and F-111) all are limited by range and would require a large aerial tanker fleet to get them to the scene of a conflict. Extended on-station time would require more tankers for force effectiveness. And basing would be a problem. Even with access to bases, supporting a US fighter squadron is an expensive and demanding proposition. Deploying Air Force squadrons to a third world country would not be like deploying to a European base where identical fighters are serviced and maintained (which is what US Air Force fighter units train to do).

At present, the US Air Force does not have techniques and doctrine appropriate for using its tactical fighter force to intervene in low-intensity conflicts. Exploring and evaluating ways to improve the ability of the Air Force to participate in low-intensity conflicts or to fight across the lower end of the conflict spectrum as the *Defense Guidance* dictates (and thus ameliorate some of the problems outlined in this chapter) is a subject worthy of serious debate by the service. This shortcoming did not always exist in the Air Force. In the early 1960s, when small wars were threatening US interests in many places, the US Air Force had a special unit that was designed to assist and integrate with third world air forces and, if necessary, intervene. It was called the Special Air Warfare Center.

NOTES

CHAPTER 5

1. AFM 2–5, *Tactical Operations Special Air Warfare*, Department of the Air Force, 22 June 1965, 14–15.
2. House Committee on Appropriations, *Hearings, Foreign Assistance and Related Agencies Appropriations for 1976*, 231–36.
3. Paul Y. Hammond, "Growing Dilemmas for the Management of Arms Sales," *Armed Forces and Society*, Fall 1979.
4. This summary of Air Force procedures for supporting mobile training teams is based on interviews with many US Air Force MTT members and with members of the Policy and Management Division, Directorate of International Programs, Deputy Chief of Staff, Programs and Resources (HQ USAF/PRIM), the tasking authority in the Air Force for obtaining US Air Force members for MTTs.
5. See Colonel Clyde E. Bodenheimer's paper, *Impact of New Technology Weapons on SAC Conventional Air Operations* (Maxwell Air Force Base, Ala.: Airpower Research Institute, 1983) for more details on the limitations of the SPF.

CHAPTER 6

EARLY LOW-INTENSITY CONFLICT EFFORTS BY THE USAF: THE SPECIAL AIR WARFARE CENTER

In contrast to the Royal Air Force experience with small wars that saw it develop a well-established and creative doctrine over a period of two decades, the US Air Force has had little cause to build a strong and enduring interest in low-intensity conflict. The history of Air Force participation in small wars is linked strongly to a very limited segment of low-intensity conflict—a role in unconventional warfare. However, the central concern in unconventional warfare is not a strategy for winning a small war, but rather a strategy for supporting regular conventional forces in a large, "hot" war. Unconventional war includes guerrilla warfare (surreptitiously introducing special warfare personnel into enemy-dominated areas), air strikes, reconnaissance, and aerial resupply and extraction of special warfare forces operating in enemy-controlled areas. It is very much more a direct-action mission that supports larger military objectives than a strategic use of specialized forces to attain specific political goals. The evolution of the Special Air Warfare Center (SAWC) illustrates the emphasis of the US Air Force on unconventional warfare and its relative lack of interest in developing long-term strategies and capabilities for low-level conflicts.

Foundation of Air Force Role in Low-Intensity Conflict

The beginning of what, in 1962, became the Special Air Warfare Center can be traced to unconventional warfare activities by early air commandos operating in China, Burma, Southeast Asia, Korea, and Europe during World War II. The ability to escape, evade, and survive in enemy-held territory was central to the mission of these early air commandos.[1]

The concept of a US air commando unit sprang from Gen H. H. Arnold's fertile imagination. He wanted to see what air power could do to support ground forces operating behind enemy lines. Thus, the mission of the 1st Air Commando Group was to support the 12,000 British troops of Brigadier Orde C. Wingate operating behind Japanese lines in Burma. Wingate's troops were placed behind the Japanese lines by air and were supplied entirely by air. The 1st Air Commando Group quickly became adept at air drops, short-field landings, evacuations, resupply, and strike missions. The group also became proficient at independent action and getting things done under the most trying of conditions. Perhaps most importantly the airmen and the men on the ground learned how to work together effectively and to develop workable joint operational plans.

In Europe effective use was made of the air commando corps, especially in resupply operations behind German lines. Operation Carpetbagger, a code name for clandestine delivery of supplies, was conceived in September 1943 with the first missions being flown in January 1944. From January to mid-September 1944, C-47s and modified B-24s of Operation Carpetbagger delivered 20,000 containers, 11,000 packages of supplies, and more than 1,000 agents behind enemy lines. The Allies began using other American transport and bomber aircraft in the spring of 1944 to deliver 160 tons of goods per month to the French forces of the interior. Thousands of guerrillas throughout Western Europe, the Mediterranean, and the Balkans were also supplied by air.

And even though the Air Force approved a program after World War II that called for the creation of seven air resupply and communications wings which would be used in unconventional warfare roles, only scant attention was paid to small wars as a separate form of conflict. Using specially configured B-29s, C-119s, SA-16s, and H-19s, these new wings were to conduct unconventional warfare, covert operations, and psychological warfare, and were to carry out clandestine intelligence collection activities. However, the Air Force commitment to these missions was not very strong. Only three of these unconventional warfare wings were able to survive budgetary cuts that were made in the early 1950s. These three remaining wings were deployed to Libya, the Philippines, and England. Only the wing assigned to the Philippines saw any combat, that coming in Korea.

In its early thinking on special operations, the Air Force focused on those tactical aspects of special air warfare that were most closely linked to unconventional operations supporting larger, conventional efforts. This tendency in Air Force thought reflected the traditional, predominant perspective subscribed to by the top officers of the Air Force. From the 1920s, US strategists thought "big." The major idea to emerge from the Air Corps Tactical School in the 1920s and 1930s was the unstoppable power of the well-planned, well-executed bomber offensive, which as a war-winning device had the potential to crush the enemy's ability and will to wage war.[2] The experience of World War II reinforced the idea that air power's role was to destroy the enemy's capacity and desire for continued conflict, and that objective was to be accomplished by massive bombing campaigns. Thus, in the minds of the Air Force leadership, there was no need to develop a small-war strategy as there had been for the British during the post-World War I era.

In Search of an Air Force Role in Small Wars

Occasionally a voice in the Air Force could be heard questioning the tremendous concentration of equipment, people, planning, and thinking that was being devoted to create a strategic force which would primarily support a massive war of annihilation beyond the scope even of World War II. One such worried voice was the Air Force vice chief of staff who, in March 1954, sent a message to the commanders of Air University, the Tactical Air Command, and the Far East Air Forces asking for comments on an issue being raised in the New Look debates then rocking the defense establishment. The vice chief felt that the New Look debates were raising doubts as to whether "air forces can do anything other than offer massive retaliatory action in the event of major war. Most of the doubts expressed and many of the outright charges made concerning limitations of the 'New Look' contain a common fundamental implication that surface forces are more capable of dealing with localized aggressions than are the air forces." The vice chief was leading up to the question he was really concerned about: What can air forces do to resolve the military problem in Indochina, where the French were doing very badly against Ho Chi Minh. The vice chief felt the Air Force did not project an ability to combat local aggression and, as a result, did not appear capable of justifying an increased emphasis upon air power to meet the military threats posed by anything short of major war.[3]

Such questions did little more than raise a flurry of activity among a few staff agencies. Serious thinking about Air Force participation in unattractive small wars did not develop—it was far too easy to concentrate on the threat of large-scale war and how the Air Force could win it in short order. It took direct prodding by the dynamic, young Kennedy administration to push the US Air Force into thinking about how air power could be applied to small wars, especially to the Communist wars of national liberation that so deeply concerned President Kennedy.

When John F. Kennedy was elected president, he expressed his dissatisfaction with Eisenhower's massive retaliation policy. He saw this policy as limiting the US reaction to Communist activity to either "indignant platitudes or an atomic bomb."[4] Kennedy believed that because of the nuclear standoff, future wars would have to be limited in nature, such as the "wars of national liberation" that Khrushchev espoused.[5] Hence a capacity for flexible response capacity was needed to counter Communist action at any level on the spectrum of conflict.

The early sixties were marked by confrontation between the superpowers—over Berlin and Cuba and in many wars of national liberation. Soviet Premier

Khrushchev pledged to support the revolutionaries in these liberation wars in a 6 April 1961 speech. He cited conflicts in Algeria, Laos, Vietnam, and Cuba as examples of increasing guerrilla activities against oppressive regimes.[6] Kennedy believed it was necessary and correct for the United States to resist aggression and Communist-inspired revolts.[7] In 1961 the National Security Council outlined policies that spelled out the US decision to counter the threat of insurgency in underdeveloped countries.[8] National Security Action Memorandum 56, May 1961, tasked the military services to develop counterinsurgency forces for special operations in their functional areas.[9]

Creation of Jungle Jim

In response, the Air Force established the 4400th Combat Crew Training Squadron (CCTS), nicknamed Jungle Jim, on 14 April 1961 at Eglin Air Force Base, Florida. Jungle Jim had a two-fold mission: training and combat. A 50-hour flying training course was given to pilots of friendly foreign air forces, and ground crews were trained to maintain aircraft under very austere conditions. Jungle Jim also provided "USAF personnel with optimum type training for supervising the development of unit combat capability in similar type aircraft of friendly foreign nations. . . ."[10] The combat mission of this new unit was divided into strike, reconnaissance, and airlift operations.

In typical fashion, the Air Force wanted this unit to be in full operation very quickly. Jungle Jim which put the Air Force into the counterinsurgency business for the first time, was to be totally operational by 8 September 1961. Everybody assigned to the unit was to to be trained on the job. They would invent the techniques and tactics of counterinsurgency in developing countries from Latin America to Africa to Southeast Asia on an ad hoc basis. There was no basic Air Force doctrine to guide them. All that the people of Jungle Jim knew was that someone on high had decreed that the Air Force would have a counterinsurgency capability, and they were it. The idea of visualizing how a small war might be planned and carried out using air power, by itself or in conjunction with other capabilities, had never been studied in the Air Force. The World War II experience of using commandos to support larger scale combat objectives did not apply to this new kind of warfare. The main thrust of the Jungle Jim mission was to impart knowledge on the capabilities of aircraft to friendly foreign forces.

The Jungle Jim units used World War II vintage aircraft such as the C-47, T-28, and B-26. These aircraft had proven their ability to operate from remote, primitive bases and had capabilities in firepower, ranges, and cargo capacities useful for counterinsurgency operations. Only four months after activation, Jungle Jim personnel made their first overseas deployment as Detachment 1 of the 4400th CCTS. Code named Sandy Beach 1, this operation involved training Mali paratroopers to operate from C-47 aircraft. It was interesting for the Jungle

Jim people to note that just across the airfield at Bamako, there stood Soviet and Czechoslovak aircraft, a stark reminder that superpower rivalry was beginning to occur in some very obscure places.[11] Detachment 1 completed its training mission in November and returned to Eglin AFB. They had established such good working relationships that air commandos returned to Mali in 1963 to give more training.

Jungle Jim's second assignment was a precursor of the conflict that would shape the role of the Air Force in small wars for years to come. In November 1961 elements from the Jungle Jim squadron (officially designated Detachment 2) went to Bien Hoa, Republic of Vietnam. Detachment 2 was nicknamed Farm Gate and the requirements of supporting it soon became central to Air Force thinking on small wars. The equipment the commandos had was not significantly different from that used by their predecessors in World War II. And, because the Air Force had not used air commandos since 1948, tactics for using the equipment came from the ingenuity and imagination of the men on the scene. Sent to Vietnam primarily to train the Vietnamese air force in counterinsurgency tactics, the men of Farm Gate from the beginning wanted to conduct an air offensive against the Vietcong. The conflict between training and combat roles for Farm Gate reflected the imprecise and often conflicting directions given to the men in the field.[12] The Kennedy administration, however, was becoming increasingly aware of the need to clarify missions and roles for the military forces involved in counterinsurgency.

The Special Air Warfare Center: Its Origin, Expansion, and Growth

In an open letter to the armed services in the spring of 1962, President Kennedy said:

> The military challenge to freedom includes the threat of war in various forms, and actual combat in many cases. We and our allies can meet the thermonuclear threat. We are building a greater "conventional deterrent capability." It remains for us to add still another military dimension: the ability to combat the threat known as guerrilla warfare.[13]

He directed the secretary of defense to "expand rapidly and substantially the orientation of existing forces for sublimited or unconventional wars."[14] In response to this political pressure, the Air Force established the Special Air Warfare Center (SAWC) at Eglin AFB on 19 April 1962. Air Force Chief of Staff Gen Curtis E. LeMay announced the creation of the new unit, which absorbed the men and assets of Jungle Jim and continued to operate Farm Gate.

The new unit was composed of the 1st Air Commando Group (1st ACG), the 1st Combat Applications Group (1st CAG), and a headquarters section (fig. 13).

THE AIR FORCE ROLE IN LOW-INTENSITY CONFLICT

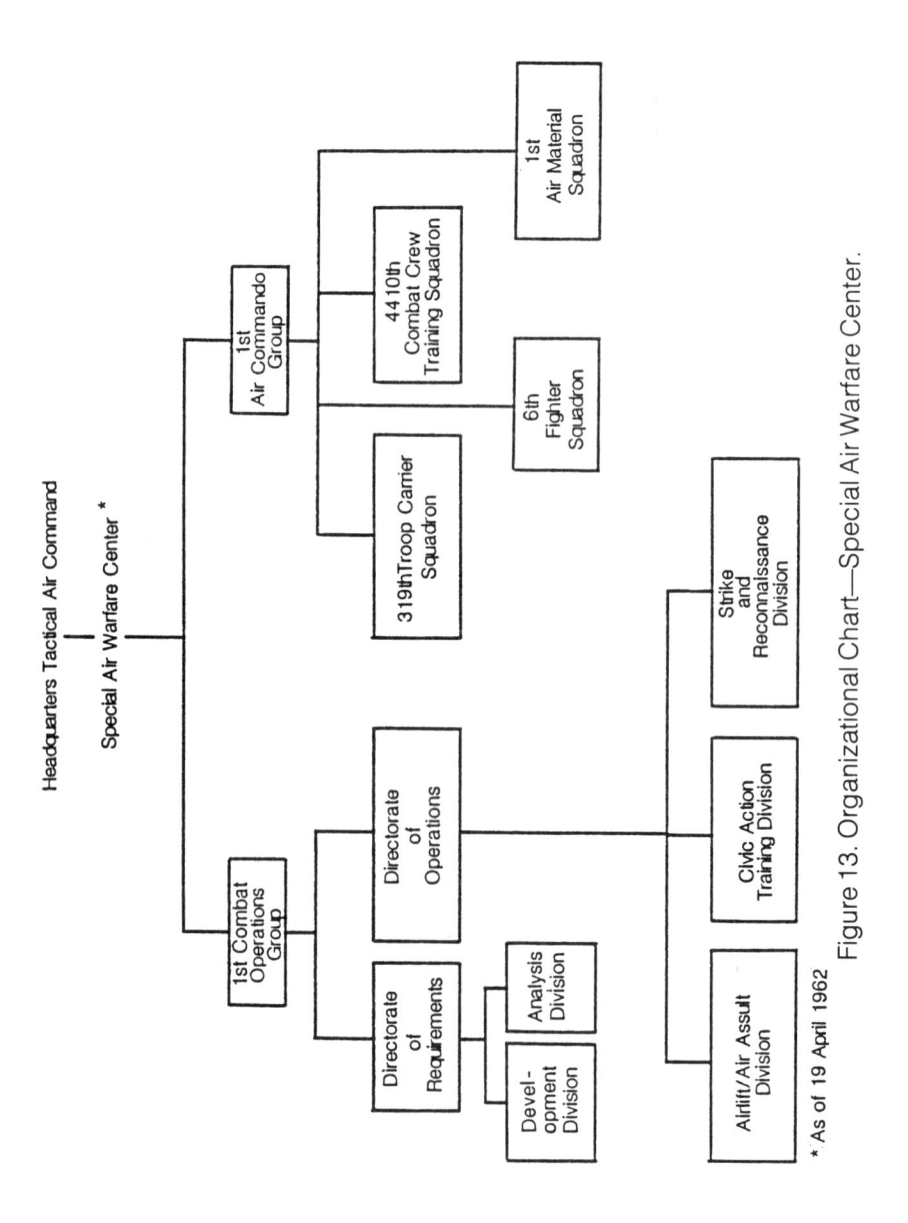

Figure 13. Organizational Chart—Special Air Warfare Center.

* As of 19 April 1962

The primary mission of SAWC was to train the air forces of friendly foreign nations in all aspects of unconventional warfare and counterinsurgency air operations and techniques. SAWC was equipped with C-47, C-46, T-28, B-26, and U-10 aircraft. The training included low-level parachute resupply, close air support, use of flares for night operations, and other counterguerrilla techniques.[15]

The 1st Combat Applications Group was a unique organization. Its task was to develop the doctrine, tactics, techniques, and hardware that the crews of the 1st Air Commando Group would use in its operations and training. The 1st CAG was responsible for all short-term development, testing, analysis, and evaluation of special operations related materiels. It could design and construct new hardware, purchase goods locally, or use and modify off-the-shelf products. If the project was too big or required more than six months to complete, it could contract out to the Air Force Systems Command (AFSC) or to civilian firms.

The period April 1962 to July 1963 was a boom time for the Special Air Warfare Center. In the first few months of its existence, the center was occupied with acquiring aircraft and equipment, becoming established at Eglin AFB and Hurlburt Field, hiring personnel, and maintaining support of its various overseas detachments. Aircrews trained in and practiced the techniques they would soon be teaching. These included assault takeoffs and landings, day and night navigation and landings, jet-assisted takeoffs in the C-47, psychological missions with leaflets and loudspeakers, flare drops, and close air support with rockets, guns, and bombs. The air commandos also received instructions in areas not normally part of air warfare: self-defense, extensive small arms training, daily physical training, and basic language training in French or Spanish. Those two languages were chosen for their wide usage in Latin America, North Africa, and Asia. Much of the vocabulary dealt with aircraft terms and words related to guerrilla warfare. Language capability was a key to success as the commandos began to operate with the air forces of the developing world.

Among the first detachments to be established after Farm Gate was Detachment 3 at Howard AFB, Canal Zone. Beginning on 10 May 1962, Detachment 3 offered counterinsurgency training to any Latin American country that requested it. Detachment 3 sent mobile training teams (MTT) throughout Latin America to survey the needs of countries that requested training. These teams determined the type of operations that it needed to conduct and gave instructions in counterinsurgency air operations and civic action techniques.

One of the key elements in the success of Detachment 3 was its civic action and training programs. Commandos from Detachment 3 provided medical assistance and evacuation in Panama and other Latin American countries. In mid-1963, the 1st Combat Applications Group developed a mobile medical dispensary. This 212-pound, three-piece unit fit easily in a U-10 light utility aircraft, and contained almost all the necessary medicines and equipment needed for ailments encountered in a tropical environment.[16] On many occasions, the air commandos of Detachment 3 flew into villages to give medical and dental care. From appendectomies to inoculations, the air commandos provided much needed treatment that had never before been available. They also conducted classes in basic hygiene for villagers. This type of civic action created much public support for the air commandos and the local government. When the air commandos conducted training for the air forces of friendly foreign countries, they pointed out to indigenous government officials that popular support could be gained from conducting such civic action operations.

Another key civic action effort was to establish regular communications with totally isolated villages. With their typical élan, the air commandos solved this difficult problem. First, a message was dropped from an airplane asking for the villagers' help in building an airstrip. Later, a U-10 equipped with loudspeakers flew over the village and instructed the villagers on how to clear the area needed for an airstrip. Once the rough strip was readied, a U-10 landed and the air commandos helped complete the strip. Later, these operations became more sophisticated, to include parachuting a tractor down to the villagers to make their task of clearing the landing site easier.

A doctrine governing the roles and mission of the commandos slowly evolved during the early period of the center's existence. SAWC's first regulation, Tactical Air Regulation 23–12, which came out on 13 July 1962, defined SAWC's mission thusly:

> [The] USAF Special Air Warfare Center will command, organize, equip, train, and administer assigned or attached forces to participate in and conduct combat improvement projects for air actions in counterinsurgency warfare and other special warfare operations.[17]

SAWC's major responsibilities included testing and evaluating projects for short-range periods, modifying existing equipment or inventing special items for special warfare, and providing forces for "supporting, instructing, and advising friendly foreign forces in counterinsurgency warfare."[18] Significantly, no mention was made of creating a capability to conduct air strikes. At this stage SAWC was merely supposed to train and develop foreign armed forces through short-term assignments overseas.[19]

By the summer of 1962 SAWC units had begun applying this emerging doctrine of assistance on a widespread scale. In August 1962 a team of air commandos from Detachment 3 went to Honduras to survey that country's needs for counterinsurgency and to train its pilots.[20] Members of Detachment 3 on another occasion installed wing racks for rockets on Guatemalan air force F-51s, resulting in a 600-percent increase in firepower.[21] Later, commandos installed radio equipment at the airfield of David, Panama, which gave the airfield necessary air traffic control capability. A year later the air commandos recovered and refinished an old ambulance and gave it to the city.[22] The air commandos flew teachers into remote areas to instruct villagers in public sanitation. They flew a US Army team into villages to drill wells and improve local agriculture. In December they airlifted Christmas gifts to cities in Panama.[23] Maj William W. McDannel, Detachment 3 commander, said:

> Civic actions are now an integral part of commando operations in Latin America. We are using the "grass roots" or people-to-people approach. In training indigenous forces, we have created many lasting friendships. These friendships inspire confidence and trust. We believe the mutual trust to be the "key" to hemispheric solidarity and the greatest deterrent to international Communism.[24]

The work of Detachment 3 clearly demonstrated that special warfare missions could be successful and showed what SAWC could accomplish with ingenuity and flexibility. Although Detachment 3's accomplishments in the remote jungles of Central America were largely overshadowed by events in Vietnam, nonetheless they had a positive impact in Central America. Looking at events today, that impact seems to have been ephemeral. One can only speculate what today's situation in Latin America would be had the kind of work being done by the commandos in 1962 been continued over the past 20 years.

In the technical arena, the 1st Combat Applications Group was busy innovating equipment to fit the mission of SAWC. From April to December 1962, the 1st CAG was involved in approximately 80 counterinsurgency, civic action, and psychological operations projects. The primary project was to modernize SAWC's air fleet. B-26s and T-28s received new engines and additional armament.[25] By 13 June 1963, the personnel of the 1st CAG had designed and installed a public address system in the C-47, C-46, and U-10 aircraft to handle psychological operations broadcasts and civic action messages.[26] The group also worked on improved methods of air resupply such as an arresting-hook delivery system—a precursor to the low-altitude parachute extraction system (LAPES).[27]

The Special Air Warfare Center continued to expand, largely because of increased commitments in Vietnam. On 1 May 1963 the center activated the 602d Fighter Squadron, which was equipped with B-26s. In July the 603d and 604th Fighter Squadrons were activated. These additions raised the 1st Air Commando Group to wing size. During this period of expansion and growth, the first indication that SAWC was not adequately performing its training mission became apparent. Farm Gate in Vietnam was supposed to be operating under Kennedy's five rules of engagement. The first of these rules, which stipulated that Vietnamese air force personnel must be aboard the aircraft on all combat support sorties, was supposed to ensure that US Air Force personnel were conducting training and were not unilaterally involved in combat. Col Joseph W. Kittenger, Jr, a B-26 pilot for Farm Gate in 1963, told, in his Corona Harvest report, how the air commandos got around this requirement. Although Vietnamese airmen were aboard these flights, they were not pilot trainees. Most of them were low-ranking enlisted men and were so unmotivated to fly that the air commandos had to take away their boots at night so they could not run away. "None of them knew anything about flying or wanted anything to do with it. . . . There was not any intention whatsoever to teach them to fly ever. They could not touch the controls if they wanted to."[28] So from the very beginning a major part of the air commando mission, training, was not being fulfilled.

Nevertheless, the air commandos did train enough pilots for two fighter squadrons. And even though an increase in the strike proficiency of the Vietnamese air force in late 1963 demonstrated that at least some training was being done, the trend for the future was set. Our training cadres were absorbed by the expanding operational effort, leaving the air commandos unable and perhaps unwilling to provide effective training. On 1 July 1963, Farm Gate was reassigned to the 2d Air Division of the Pacific Air Forces (PACAF). The Special Air Warfare Center still trained the aircrews going to Vietnam, but for operational and administrative purposes Farm Gate was run by PACAF. This move removed a vital element of its forces from the control of the Special Air Warfare Center.[29]

The experience of Farm Gate nonetheless provided the basis for planning future assistance missions in the third world. Brig Gen Gilbert L. Pritchard, commander of the Special Air Warfare Center, wrote, in his 1963 commander's appraisal, that the use of mobile training teams to assist newly emerging and independent nations in their fight against emerging and independent nations in their fight against "subversive insurgency" would continue to grow in importance. He noted that "today, as a result of our evaluation of the potential of this program, this command is now prepared and has in being specially trained and equipped military training teams to meet the future demands of the unified commands for such assistance."[30] Thinking about using commando resources in situations after Vietnam was clearly alive at Hurlburt Field, Florida, in spite of the immediate requirements of that conflict.

A Time of Organizational Change

With the transfer of Detachment 2 (Farm Gate) to PACAF, the Special Warfare Center entered a period of organizational change. New units were established and old ones expanded. The Vietnam conflict had its greatest impact on the organization during this time.

On 25 July 1963 the Joint Chiefs of Staff indicated that they wanted a special air warfare squadron in Europe. In response Detachment 4 was established at Sembach Air Base, Germany, in January 1964. Detachment 4 could conduct day or night resupply and air drops, psychological operations, and photo-documentation missions and could provide mobile training teams.[31]

On 1 August 1963, the Tactical Air Command published a new regulation that redefined the center's mission to meet the needs of the expanding organization. Now SAWC would command, organize, equip, train, administer, *and, in special instances, operate assigned or attached forces for the purpose of conducting air actions in counterinsurgency,* counterguerilla warfare, unconventional, and psychological warfare. In addition, the Special Air Warfare Center will conduct combat improvement projects designed to increase the effectiveness of all air operations associated with special warfare.[32] [Emphasis added.]

The center was given two major responsibilities. The first was training, deploying, and, in special instances, employing special air warfare (SAW) forces in counterinsurgency. The second covered the 1st Combat Applications Group's duties, which included testing and evaluating items or systems in short-range periods, devising or modifying equipment, and developing doctrine, tactics, and techniques for SAWC operations. The center also had responsibilities to establish liaison with Army, Navy, and Air National Guard special warfare units.

A significant difference between this and the previous regulation was that SAWC was now authorized

through application of airpower and associated resources [to] optimize air-ground operations with indigenous military and/or irregular forces engaged in counterinsurgency operations either unilaterally or in conjunction with other US military or government agencies.[33]

The new regulation now authorized the Special Air Warfare Center to conduct strike combat operations, which, early in 1962, Washington had admitted Farm Gate was doing anyway.[34]

In the same time frame, the center developed an interesting new concept as reflected in SAWC Op-plan 5-63. Under this plan, the center was to develop a special air warfare force that could deploy within 24 hours to any selected area of the world. Once there, this force would be able to operate in conjunction with and in support of US or friendly forces in counterinsurgency, unconventional warfare, and psychological warfare operations. It was also to provide training to a friendly nation's air forces in those areas.[35] Clearly, the center had a considerable material and intellectual investment in providing an air force capability in a wide range of small wars.

But this capability never came to full fruition due to the increasing demands of Vietnam. Because of the quantum increases in strike and airlift requirements for special air warfare assets in Southeast Asia, the role of SAWC more and more shifted to training US Air Force crews and away from its mission of providing combat- and advisory-ready forces. General Pritchard noted that

utilization of nearly all of the strike resources of the center by the conduct of an accelerated training program completely divested the center of a capability to provide combat ready strike forces for support of US Strike Command and other unified command contingency requirements.[36]

The Special Air Warfare Center was quickly becoming a very busy training center with the "special" part of its title being replaced by the routine demands of an expanding conventional war in Vietnam.

Late 1963 and early 1964 was an extremely busy time for SAWC. The center had grown from a small unit with limited resources to almost 3,000 personnel spread throughout the world, a growing inventory of aircraft, and funding priority for its test projects. New detachments were established, mobile training teams were sent out, and major organizational changes took place.

The chief of staff, Air Force, wanted to start a special air warfare unit for the Middle East, Africa, and South Asia; it was to be assigned to Strike Command. In response SAWC established Detachment 5 on 11 February 1964, but it was not operationally ready for some time.[37] Detachment 5 (Provisional), known as Tiger Rag, was to be capable of reacting quickly and deploying with Strike Command forces. The unit was stationed at Hurlburt Field, Florida.

Another unit, Detachment 6 (Water Pump) was sent to Udorn, Thailand, in January 1964, to train the Laotian air force in counterinsurgency to provide a nucleus of US counterinsurgency forces near Laos for combat operations, and to stimulate the Royal Thai Air Force to step up its counterinsurgency program.[38] At first the detachment was equipped with a small number of T-28s; later it received C-47s as well.

During mid-July 1964 the Special Air Warfare Center continued its pattern of organizational change. Events in Vietnam directly affected the organization. On 1 July 1964, Detachment 3 in Panama, which had been renamed the 605th Air Commando Squadron (Composite), passed to Southern Command's control.[39] Detachment 3's operations were the benchmark of how effective a good SAWC program could be. This unit had provided many highly successful civic action programs and counterinsurgency training to various Latin American countries. The removal of this unit from SAWC's control severely curtailed the center's role in training foreign forces. Now the only active training detachment of SAWC was Detachment 6 (Water Pump) in Thailand. In contrast, the major contribution of Detachment 5 (Tiger Rag), a CONUS-based unit, was to Strike Command exercises, while Detachment 4 in Germany provided unconventional warfare support to United States Air Forces, Europe. Toward the end of 1964, activities of the center's mobility training teams had all but ceased.

At this juncture, SAWC proposed a reorganization to the Tactical Air Command. The center wanted one large consolidated unit to conduct training. The proposal also included the radical combination of strike and airlift units into composite squadrons. This reorganization would make it easier to accommodate the increased load of training aircrews at Hurlburt. On 27 July 1964, the TAC commander, Gen Walter C. Sweeney, Jr, approved part of this reorganization. He accepted the formation of a composite training squadron but not the reorganization of the operational training squadrons into three composite strike or airlift squadrons. In October, the 4410th Combat Crew Training Squadron was activated.[40]

At the end of December 1964 General Pritchard, the commander of SAWC, described four areas of responsibility in the center's mission. First, the center was to develop doctrine and tactics for air aspects of counterinsurgency, unconventional warfare, and psychological operations. Second, SAWC was to train and equip US forces in the strike, reconnaissance, and airlift roles of special air warfare. Third, the center was to provide advice and assistance in training indigenous forces. Last, SAWC was to provide air support to the Army's Special Forces. This step in the evolution of SAWC's mission placed its training of foreign air forces as third priority.

In January 1965, the mission statement of the 1st Combat Applications Group's for the first time, failed to mention the development of doctrine.[41] Although this group did provide data to aircrews in Vietnam on how to best dive bomb with World War II vintage aircraft and how to avoid flak, most of its efforts went to developing hardware for air commando units rather than to doctrine or tactics. This situation resulted because the 1st CAG was undermanned and staffed mostly with technical people. Almost no attempt had been made to establish any doctrine or correct tactics for counterinsurgency warfare; operational units were sent into the field to develop their own methods for counterinsurgency. For the most part, these units used conventional air power tactics, especially in Vietnam, and, to a lesser extent, elsewhere.

The center tried to keep alive the idea of specialized people to work foreign assistance. In January 1965 it had the opportunity to comment on a draft document called the "Air Force Plan." The plan apparently was a philosophical analysis of the future direction of the Air Force. The center pointed out two basic concerns, which were prophetic—it conceded that preventing war on a grand scale was clearly the Air Force's primary concern, but it also warned that the Air Force should not ignore subversion in the free countries of the developing world. Specifically the center noted that "the nation-building capability of the Air Force and its ability to train friendly air forces through the use of military training teams has not been clearly stated as a capability or clearly established as a requirement." Further, the plan apparently lumped all nonnuclear, nonstrategic forces into a conventional capability. However, the center believed that in the normal course of duty, pilots (fighter or transport) lacked the "talent" and experience required for military assistance, civic action, and nation-building. As early as 1965, the erosion of the idea of a specialized force to accomplish US Air Force to foreign air force training was well established.[42] Even though the war in Vietnam had expanded far beyond a counterinsurgency operation, SAWC people still held to the idea that sending specially trained detachments to indoctrinate the air forces of friendly foreign countries on how to employ air power was a valid concept particularly where conditions were different from Vietnam—that is, where the conflict had not graduated to a full-scale conventional war. The growing emphasis on training combat crews in the mid-sixties, however, forced the center to devote more and more of its resources into the business of training people for the larger war in Vietnam. By 1966 SAWC had become primarily

> a combat training unit, preparing people for Air Force commands and a number of friendly foreign powers . . . rather than training and maintaining combat ready forces in being for counterinsurgency or civic action missions in all parts of the world.[43]

Vietnam Devours Special Air Warfare Center Assets

As 1965 drew to an end, the Vietnam War had its most telling impact on the Special Air Warfare Center. Trained aircrews were needed to resupply the expanding effort in Vietnam, and SAWC was the unit to provide these crews. In a major organizational change, the 1st Air Commando Wing (1st ACW) was moved to England AFB, Louisiana, and the 4410th Combat Crew Training Squadron was expanded to a wing at Hurlburt.[44] The departure of 1st ACW relieved some of the congestion at Hurlburt caused by the expansion of existing units and provided more room for aircrew training. Now the number one mission of the Special Air Warfare Center was to train and equip aircrews and ground crews for operations in Vietnam. Officially the Tactical Air Command (TAC) still required the center to provide mobile training teams to unified commands to train friendly foreign air forces in counterinsurgency, but this requirement was ignored both by TAC and the center as training US aircrews became SAWC's big mission.[45] By late 1966 the war had clearly escalated to a conventional level. The air commandos were not involved in counterguerrilla operations, but mostly conducted close air support operations in support of the conventional war.[46]

On 8 July 1968 SAWC was redesignated the US Air Force special operations force (SOF), and became the equivalent of a numbered air force. Yet, as operations in Vietnam became more conventional, the need for the Special Operations Force lessened and the command billet was reduced from a major general to a brigadier general. The reduction in rank was incongruous with an apparent increase in organizational statute from the unique designation of a center to the organizational equivalent of a numbered air force.

As the Vietnam effort wound down, beginning in late 1969, the SOF was gradually squeezed by budgetary and manpower cutbacks. By 1970 SOF unit manning was at 30 percent. The decline in assets continued space through the early seventies; on 30 June 1974 the special operations force was deactivated, officially closing out this important chapter on special operations within the Air Force. The final unit history notes the passing of the organization:

> This is the final installment of the history of the USAF Special Operations Force, an elite element of the Tactical Air Command. Changing priorities, the ever-trimming budget scalpel,

and shrinking manpower resources were the key factors in the decision to deactivate the USAF Special Operations Force.[47]

Lessons from the Special Air Warfare Center

Even a cursory look at the history and activities of the Special Air Warfare Center suggests some points about early Air Force participation in low-intensity conflict. First, it is clear that the center was created in response to political pressure from the top. Without President Kennedy's call to create forces to fight Communist-sponsored wars of national liberation, it seems very unlikely that the Air Force would have generated a counterinsurgent capability on its own. Second, the center was created in rapid order. Aircraft and men were thrown together hurriedly and with there was no time to develop thinking on strategies and doctrines that could guide the plans of those earliest Air Force counterinsurgent forces. As noted by Col Robert Gleason, who was with the commandos from Jungle Jim days, "The immediate missions of the original USAF COIN unit (Jungle Jim) . . . were not immediately obvious even to the original cadre."[48] The organization, equipment, planning, and developing concepts of operation for the early air commandos was very much an ad hoc affair.

The importance of doctrine in this case must be stressed. A lack of doctrine and the short time between SAWC's inception and its first operations are the keys to the problem that resulted in the misuse of this special organization. The Special Air Warfare Center was entering a brand new field beyond any experience of the Air Force and most of the military. Entering the counterinsurgency arena without guidance encouraged the use of conventional air power tactics. The British air control methods of the 1920s and 1930s, psychological operations, and civic actions, such as using loudspeaker operations to guide the construction of airstrips, are examples of unconventional uses of air power that could have been applied in Vietnam. However, as early as 1963, the Commander in Chief of the Pacific Command, Adm Harry D. Felt, noted that Farm Gate fliers were conducting conventional missions and did not need counterinsurgency training.[49]

In spite of the lack of conceptual thinking that went into establishing Air Force counterinsurgency forces in the early sixties the people assigned to that task did a most impressive job in establishing a credible force. The basic idea of developing a force to impart techniques and training to friendly foreign air forces took root quickly. Aircraft were obtained that were simple and rugged enough to operate under primitive conditions. A separate organization was created to obtain and develop equipment for use in developing countries. People were trained in languages, cross-cultural relations, hand-to-hand combat, and a host of other skills not normally part of an Air Force career. Operating outside the bounds of usual Air Force operations became normal for the air commandos. A sense of "eliteness" came naturally to the air commandos because of their special training, special missions, and special way of operating.

The success of the 1st Combat Applications Group in providing counterinsurgency and civic action equipment for the 1st Air Commando Wing gave the center a unique resource. The group also gave the center flexibility to handle the unusual missions that came its way. The 1st Combat Applications Group completed literally thousands of projects from 1962 to 1972, ranging between testing the prototype VC-123 transport under field conditions and designing an efficient way to dispense sterile screwworm flies. The group developed low-light-level television equipment for night strikes and reconnaissance and cargo extraction systems. It also designed and tested the AC-47, -119, and -130 gunship platforms. The technical requirements of operating in a counterinsurgent and small war environment taxed the ingenuity and resources of this organization. But its ability to function quickly to find ways to get the job done by going beyond routine Air Force supply and research and development channels was legendary.

The Special Air Warfare Center also scored many successes with its mobile training teams and civic action programs. Our air commandos contributed to the capacity of third world militaries to function effectively, and showed them how to improve both the conditions in their countries and the relations with their citizens. By operating with and magnifying the role of the host nation's military in civic action programs, the commando teams increased the prestige of the local military in the eyes of its own population. Also, the US assistance in conducting beneficial programs provided a boost to the prestige of the United States in remote areas throughout the world. Often teams served as a bridge between army and air force hierarchies in third world countries. In many of these countries, the army and air force were (and remain today) distinct competitors. This competition resulted in complete breakdown in communication. By conducting joint training operations, the air commandos were able to bridge the communications gap and establish a good working relationship between these indigenous forces. Our air commandos contributed to the capability of third world militaries to function effectively, and showed them how to improve both the conditions in their countries and the relations with their citizens. The benefits of these low-risk, low-cost operations were continued friendship and respect as well as possible direct military benefits, such as basing agreements. Due to the increased commitments to Vietnam, these efforts declined dramatically.

As the Vietnam War grew, the center's mission eventually underwent a dramatic change. In its original inception, the Special Air Warfare Center had conducted operations worldwide and had had considerable control over its own operations. But as US involvement in Southeast Asia intensified, special operations in Vietnam soon ceased to be "special." As Colonel Gleason noted, the Vietnam War quickly erased the distinction between special air warfare and conventional air force assets, the only difference being the "age of the aircraft assigned to each."[50] Conventional tactics such as interdiction, close air support, and reconnaissance became the mainstay of Farm Gate's operations. The special capabilities of SAWC's personnel were becoming more and more limited by their assignment to the increasingly narrow role of combat training. By 1973, the mission of the Special Air Warfare Center had officially narrowed the role of training and operating forces in Air Force special operations, and to training other US Air Force and allied personnel as directed by Headquarters Tactical Air Command or Headquarters USAF. The center's previously wide-ranging responsibilities had fallen completely by the wayside.

Thus, because of the demands of Vietnam, the Special Air Warfare Center never had the time to develop and prove an air doctrine that operated outside the bounds of normal, conventional air tactics. Moreover, as the Vietnam War wound down, the Air Force quickly pulled back from any commitment to a special operations force. After the war the Special Operations Force was disbanded with most of its assets being sent to various elements of the Tactical Air Command. What few assets remained were quickly committed to the narrow, unconventional warfare mission of supporting conventional operations by operating behind enemy lines and by carrying out specific one-time missions. For the past 12 years, the Air Force special operations capability has been only a faint shadow of its mid-1960s force of over 5,000 men and women and 550 aircraft. The force has dwindled to one wing based in the United States (the 1st Special Operations Wing), which operates four types of aircraft—the AC-130 Spectre gunship, the MC-130 Combat Talon, the HH-53 Pave Low, and the UH-1N helicopter. Two other operational Combat Talon squadrons operate overseas. Altogether there are only 37 aircraft in the active Air Force special operations inventory. The shortage of equipment is, however, only the tip of the iceberg when one considers the organizational, doctrinal, and philosophical issues that are as yet unresolved in the Air Force concerning the mission of the Air Force in small wars in general and in low-intensity conflict specifically.

NOTES

CHAPTER 6

1. The sketch that follows is based on a historical review of Air Force unconventional warfare activities sent by General Walter C. Sweeney, Jr, commander, Tactical Air Command, to General John K. Waters, commanding general, United States Continental Army Command, 19 July 1963.
2. See R. F. Futrell, *Ideas, Concepts, Doctrine: A History of Basic Thinking in the United States Air Force, 1907-1964*, AU-19 (Maxwell AFB, Ala.: Air University, 1974), 31-47.
3. HQ USAF, Chief of Staff message DTG 302128Z, March 1954.
4. R. Montgomery, *Military Civic Action and Counterinsurgency: The Birth of a Policy* (Ann Arbor, Mich.: University Microfilms, 1971), 24.
5. Ibid., 28.
6. Ibid., 20.
7. Richard J. Walton, *Cold War and Counterrevolution: The Foreign Policy of John F. Kennedy* (New York: Viking Press, 1972).
8. R. L. Gleason, "Quo Vadis?—The Nixon Doctrine and Air Power," *Air University Review* 23, no. 5 (July-August 1972): 49.
9. Walton, *Cold War and Counterrevolution*, 169.
10. USAF Special Air Warfare Center (TAC), *History*, vol. 2 (27 April-31 December 1962), "Jungle Jim Final Operational Concept," supporting document 7. In USAF Historical Collection, USAF Historical Research Center, Maxwell AFB, Ala.
11. Brig Gen Jamie Gough, "Airpower and Counter-insurgency," *Airman* 6, no. 8 (August 1962): 2-7.
12. Robert F. Futrell, *The United States Air Force in Southeast Asia: The Advisory Years to 1965* (Washington, D.C.: Office of Air Force History, 1981), 83-84.
13. USAF Special Air Warfare Center (TAC), *History*, 1 April-31 December 1962, 1:14. In USAF Historical Collection, USAF Historical Research Center, Maxwell AFB, Ala.
14. John Hawkins Napier III, "The Air Commandos in Vietnam, Nov 5 1961-Feb 7 1965" (unpublished thesis, Auburn University, 16 March 1967).
15. *Air Force Times*, 5 May 1962, 1.
16. Ibid., 31 July 1963, 21.
17. USAF Special Air Warfare Center (TAC), *History*, 1 April-31 December 1962, vol. 2, supporting document 8, 1. In USAF Historical Collection, USAF Historical Research Center, Maxwell AFB, Ala.
18. Ibid., 2.

19. USAF Special Air Warfare Center (TAC), *History*, 1 April–31 December 1962, 1:212.
20. Ibid., 220.
21. Ibid., 229.
22. USAF Special Air Warfare Center (TAC), *History*, 1 January–30 June 1963, 1:148. In USAF Historical Collection, USAF Historical Research Center, Maxwell AFB, Ala.
23. Ibid., 234.
24. USAF Special Air Warfare Center (TAC), *History*, 1 April–31 December 1962, 1:245.
25. Ibid., 303.
26. Ibid., 306.
27. USAF Special Air Warfare Center (TAC), *History*, 1 January–30 June 1964, vol. 2, appendix K, A2–7. In USAF Historical Collection, USAF Historical Research Center, Maxwell AFB, Ala.
28. USAF Oral History Program, Col Joseph W. Kittenger, Jr, interview, 5 September 1974, 24–25 (U). In USAF Historical Research Center, Maxwell AFB, Ala.
29. Ibid., 12.
30. Ibid., 21.
31. USAF Special Air Warfare Center (TAC), *History*, 1 January–30 June 1965, supporting document 3. In USAF Historical Collection, USAF Historical Research Center, Maxwell AFB, Ala.
32. USAF Special Air Warfare Center (TAC), *History*, 1 January–30 June 1966, "Foreword." In USAF Historical Collection, USAF Historical Research Center, Maxwell AFB, Ala.
33. USAF Special Air Warfare Center (TAC), *History*, 1 January–30 June 1965, 9.
34. USAF Special Air Warfare Center (TAC), *History*, 1 July–31 December 1965, 14. In USAF Historical Collection, USAF Historical Research Center, Maxwell AFB, Ala.
35. Ibid., 1.
36. *Air Force Times*, 2 November 1966, 26.
37. USAF Special Air Warfare Center (TAC), *History*, 1 July 1973–30 June 1974, "Foreword." In USAF Historical Collection, USAF Historical Research Center, Maxwell AFB, Ala.
38. Gleason, "Quo Vadis?", 23 and 49.
39. Futrell, *The USAF in Southeast Asia: The Advisory Years to 1965*, 170.
40. Gleason, "Quo Vadis?", 23 and 49.
41. USAF Special Air Warfare (TAC), *History*, 1 January–30 June 1965, supporting document 3. In USAF Historical Collection, USAF Historical Research Center, Maxwell AFB, Ala.
42. USAF Special Air Warfare Center (TAC), *History*, 1 January–30 June 1966, "Foreword." In USAF Historical Collection, USAF Historical Research Center, Maxwell AFB, Ala.
43. USAF Special Air Warfare Center (TAC), *History* 1 January–30 June 1965, 9.
44. USAF Special Air Warfare Center (TAC), *History*, 1 July–31 December 1965, 14. In USAF Historical Collection, USAF Historical Research Center, Maxwell AFB, Ala.
45. Ibid., 1.
46. *Air Force Times*, 2 November 1966, 26.
47. USAF Special Air Warfare Center (TAC), *History*, 1 July 1973–30 June 1974, "Foreword." In USAF Historical Collection, USAF Historical Research Center, Maxwell AFB, Ala.
48. Gleason, "Quo Vadis?", 23 and 49.
49. Futrell, *The USAF in Southeast Asia: The Advisory Years to 1965*, 170.
50. Gleason, "Quo Vadis?", 23 and 49.

CHAPTER 7

A PLAN FOR USAF PARTICIPATION IN LOW-INTENSITY CONFLICT

If the Air Force is to be an effective instrument of national power in low-intensity conflict, it must recognize the peculiar difficulties of war at the lower reaches of the conflict spectrum and commit a modest portion of its intellectual and material resources to building a low-intensity capability. Some of the fundamental problems that make participating in low-intensity conflicts difficult include the seemingly nebulous interests of the Unites States in becoming involved in such conflicts, the difficulty of obtaining public support for assistance or intervention in the third world, the difficulty of clearly defining precise US objectives, and the reluctance of military leaders to develop special capabilities for unfamiliar kinds of conflict.[1] That is, reallocating funds and shifting priorities away from the mainstream efforts of the military (strategic nuclear deterrence, fighting a major conventional war in Europe, and protecting the oil fields of the Middle East) are difficult for the military. Hence, the US military tends to depend on conventional force structures, conventional command structures, and conventionally trained and equipped forces to cope with small wars. As the Morocco case study points out, important political and military constraints impinge on any US effort to assist a friendly third world country. Intervening in any form in the third world results in similar difficulties. The US Air Force, to be effective in such situations, must have very detailed knowledge about the recipient of US assistance and the capabilities and limitations of that nation's military forces. Only after the Air Force recognizes that participating in low-intensity conflicts requires special knowledge and special capabilities can the debate begin on how best to organize and develop that capability.

Committing the Organization

The Air Force seemingly puts a good deal of emphasis on its low-intensity capability by highlighting the importance of the USAF special operations forces—forces theoretically tailored for low-intensity conflict. The basic doctrine of the Air Force (Air Force Manual [AFM] 1–1, *Basic Aerospace Doctrine of the United States Air Force*, 16 March 1984), lists special operations as one of the nine basic operational missions of the United States Air Force. Because it is one of the basic operational missions, commanders are required to prepare their forces for that mission. Yet, the special operations mission in AFM 1–1 is defined vaguely as "operations which are undertaken in enemy controlled or politically sensitive territory, cover a broad spectrum of action and are conducted at every level of conflict."[2] The Air Force recognizes unconventional warfare, foreign internal defense (FID), and psychological warfare as the three main facets of special operations, but in spelling them out it suggests that these roles are limited in scope to short-term or one-shot efforts. For example, AFM 1–1 states that the evasion and escape, guerrilla warfare, sabotage, direct action missions, and other covert or clandestine operations associated with unconventional warfare missions are to be directed "by the joint unconventional warfare task force of a unified command for military, political, economic, and ideological purposes." Thus, the unconventional warfare mission refers almost exclusively to activity behind enemy lines, implying that it is a mission adjunct only to those undertaken in a conventional conflict. Likewise, US forces assigned to the role of foreign internal defense will have only an ad hoc mission of assisting "allied or friendly nations in maintaining their internal defense operations." Forces assigned to this mission "are often sent into unstable areas to help the host country to prevent low-level conflict from expanding into open hostility" through such programs "as education, training, and military construction." Finally, those forces that are to conduct or support psychological warfare are expected to operate only behind enemy lines and against hostile forces by developing "comprehensive programs to influence favorably the attitudes and behavior of hostile forces and people in areas under enemy control."[3] The idea of creating forces that can operate on a long-term basis to do things such as help a third world air force grow effectively, to integrate with an air force already involved in a conflict, or to intervene directly in a conflict in support of US policy goals is not accommodated by that part of the Air Force's basic doctrine which comes closest to considering the issue of low-intensity conflict, namely, special operations.

Another way to judge the commitment of the Air Force to its various missions is the emphasis given to efforts to procure, maintain, and improve the equipment dedicated to each mission. The intense effort to get substantial numbers of the B-1, MX, F-15, and F-16 shows rather clearly the importance the Air Force attaches to its strategic attack and air superiority missions. Special operations has been given little attention in recent years. In fact, it has been called by many of those in special operations the "forgotten force."[4] In contrast, during its heyday in the early 1960s, the Special Air Warfare Center had 550 aircraft capable of performing several special operations missions, including reconnaissance, aerial resupply, forward air control, close air support, and interdiction. The aircraft were designed to operate from unimproved airfields, could be supported by host country air forces, and were operated by men specifically trained in assisting third world air forces.

Today, however, this large, capable force has dwindled to a mere 37 active duty aircraft thinly spread between the 1st Special Operations Wing at Hurlburt Field, Florida, and two overseas squadrons at Rhein-Main AB, Germany, and Clark AB, Philippines; these two units operate the MC-130 Combat Talon. The wing at Hurlburt also operates the AC-130 Spectre gunship, the HH-53 Pave Low helicopter, and the UH-1N helicopter. These aircraft are uniquely capable in many ways, yet are able to perform only a narrow range of missions.

The MC-130 Combat Talon is specifically designed and equipped to support long-range infiltration, extraction, and aerial resupply and to do so in spite of any type of enemy air defenses. This aircraft also has a limited photo reconnaissance capability. The AC-130 Spectre is the only aircraft in special operations capable of delivering firepower. And since it is equipped with infrared, television, and radar sensors to acquire targets and pinpoint friendly forces, the AC-130 can operate as effectively at night as it can in daylight. Armed with 20-mm, 40-mm, and 105-mm guns, it is ideal for missions that require very accurate fire, such as supporting troops in contact with the enemy, perimeter defense, and search and destroy missions. Special operations helicopters allow support of missions where prepared airfields are not available.[5]

But this handful of aircraft assigned to special operations gives the Air Force the ability to participate in low-intensity conflict only in a very limited way. The missions for which the US Air Force special operations force is presently configured are direct-action, one-time raids such as the aborted Iran rescue attempt. Capabilities for the broader missions of low-intensity conflict—assisting third world air forces, integrating with them, or directly intervening in a situation that requires activity beyond a single mission—are not currently within the means of the Air Force special operations force. Furthermore, limiting Air Force special operations to direct-action missions may soon become part of Air Force doctrine and policy. A January 1983 draft of AFM 1-1 defines special operations as a *combat mission* conducted to exploit counteroffensive actions through low-visibility covert or clandestine actions across the spectrum of conflict. The draft further states that the Air Force special operations force can conduct and support direct-action counterterrorist operations, collective security, psychological operations, and humanitarian operations.[6] The implication of this definition is that special operations are basically reactive in nature since they primarily exploit counteroffensive actions. However, the thrust of participating in low-intensity conflict is that forces must be able to act in several ways; to be effective they must not be committed only for one-time missions.

While direct-action missions have remained a recognizable part of Air Force special operations, the two other aspects of its mission—foreign internal defense and psychological operations—have been grossly neglected. Although the proposed draft of AFM 1-1 does not mention foreign internal defense as an Air Force mission, it does mention "collective security" as falling under special operations' area of responsibility. ("Collective security" is not defined in the draft AFM 1-1, so it could have the same meaning as foreign internal defense.) Foreign internal defense, however, remains on the books as a mission for the special operations force. For example, Tactical Air Command Manual (TACM) 2-1, *Tactical Air Operations,* says foreign internal defense (FID)

> operations are conducted on request from a foreign government and are to aid allied nations to attain an established label of military self-reliance. . . . The role of USAF SOFs in FID is to encourage, advise, and train indigenous personnel in nation building and internal security activities.[7]

Moreover, participating in foreign internal defense operations is the heart of the assistance level of activity postulated earlier. Such activity would dominate operations in the areas of noncombat force employment, advisory assistance, and providing cadre for host forces (fig. 3, chap. 1). Assisting the air forces of friendly countries can take a wide variety of forms but, in any form, it is a complex undertaking. Some of the goals of an assistance mission could include providing security for US-owned assets against threatened insurgent activity, maintaining a friendly government in power, gaining strategic access to a region to obtain basing or port rights, securing access to resources in a region, or related aims.

However, the intended recipient often will have problems with accepting US military assistance. Some countries may be reluctant to request US military assistance for fear that the presence of US personnel could cast doubt on the patriotism and independence of the regime. Such an attitude could make establishing a long-term air force to air force relationship difficult. Hence, we must be able to anticipate problem areas; acting early will be equally crucial. On the other hand, when a third world nation is facing pressing internal or external threats, its government is much more likely to seek assistance. A request for help in what has become a crisis situation means that the United States must be able to make a quickly planned, organized, and coordinated response. Thus, our resources must be committed to a situation that not only may involve active combat but also brings with it the risk of casualties, propaganda attacks on the

US government, and media coverage that might result in a negative public reaction in the United States, which in turn would make the assistance attempt even more difficult to pursue successfully.

Effective psychological warfare in low-intensity conflict is perhaps even more difficult than foreign internal defense operations. As mentioned earlier, psychological warfare operations should be part of any military operation, regardless of the level of intensity. They should condition populations in a target area to support specific US assistance efforts, subvert, enemy forces, and, on a long-term basis, generate favorable perceptions toward US policies and interests on a regional basis.

But developing a capacity for psychological operations is very difficult. The military forces involved must receive detailed training in psychology, mass-media techniques, communications, and cross-cultural relations, plus an interdisciplinary understanding of the target population's history and cultural, religious, economic, political, and military values. The Air Force has never developed the intellectual resources to design true psychological warfare operations of any scale. Moreover, even though TAC Manual 2–1 includes psychological operations (PSYOPS) as a mission for the Air Force special operations force, the Air Force's role in psychological operations has been primarily in the area of disseminating information. As *Air Force 2000* states, "PSYOP responsibilities are primarily an Army rather than an Air Force function. The proper Air Force role should be covert dissemination of PSYOP broadcasts and programs."[8] Yet there are important potential roles for the Air Force in psychological warfare, as will be discussed shortly.

The Air Force is currently at a low point in its ability to accomplish its special operations mission in the areas of unconventional warfare, foreign internal defense, and psychological warfare. In addition to the drawdown of its aircraft assets, the special operations mission has suffered from weak interest within the Air Force as suggested by Deputy Assistant Secretary of Defense for International Security Affairs Noel Koch at an Air War College symposium in 1985.[9]

In 1982 with capabilities for participating in low-intensity conflict at such a low point, the Air Force saw the need to realign completely the command structure for the special operations force. The Tactical Air Command had controlled special operations assets since the days of Jungle Jim and the Special Air Warfare Center. Under TAC, special operations in the Air Force saw both its days of greatest activity and expansion and its long recent history of neglect and contraction. Moreover, because of the unique and specialized kind of warfare to which they were dedicated, special operations people in TAC were always outside the mainstream of Tactical Air Command thinking. And being equipped with a strange mixture of aircraft, none of which resemble fast-moving F-15s and F-16s, the special operations units in TAC were distinctly out of place. These factors may have contributed to the precipitous decline in the capability of the special operations force since the Vietnam War. The reorganization of the special operations force that was approved in December 1982 and took effect on 1 March 1983 places all special operations forces under the Military Airlift Command. The special operations force was elevated from a wing to an air division. The Aerospace Rescue and Recovery Service (ARRS), long a MAC organization, also became an air division and was joined with the special operations force to form a new numbered air force, the Twenty-Third Air Force.

This reorganization means nothing in terms of additional manpower and equipment for the special operations force. It could be, however, the first step in a renaissance of special operations in the Air Force. MAC is a global command with global responsibilities, while TAC is a continental command that has training and readiness as its primary missions. MAC has also been very supportive of the special mission of the ARRS. Indeed, as the most decorated unit to come out of the Vietnam War, ARRS has long been a source of pride for the Military Airlift Command. Perhaps, under the Military Airlift Command the deficiencies of the current special operations force will be corrected. The time seems auspicious for a rebirth of special air warfare.

Doctrine and Philosophy

The first step in such a renaissance is to establish a new philosophy for special operations in the Air Force and to develop the doctrine that will be the basis for establishing a force structure that meets the need of the philosophy. The philosophy for participating in low-intensity conflict is very simple. It should recognize that applying power in low-intensity conflicts is a complex undertaking that includes a wide range of activity in small conflicts. The service must recognize that participating in low-intensity conflicts may be a long-term affair, could have very limited political goals, and may require operating with minimal fanfare. There likely will be little "glory" for low-intensity warriors and no great air campaigns. Rather, air power in low-intensity conflicts must be used as required to achieve a clearly defined political goal, whether it be to build an air capability in a friendly nation's armed forces, to stabilize and support a regime threatened by external aggression, or to apply military pressure directly in support of US political objectives.

The philosophy, then, should not be based on discrete kinds of missions epitomized by the unconventional warfare, foreign internal defense, and psychological warfare missions that currently make up special operations. Rather the philosophy should be to apply the right level of assistance, integration of forces, or intervention appropriate to the situation (unconventional warfare, foreign internal defense, or psychological warfare) to achieve the objective. Thus, Air Force participation in low-intensity conflict needs to be considered in terms of assistance, integration of forces, and intervention. And the Air Force must develop, from a philosophic base that postulates the limited goals and specialized means applicable to low-intensity conflict, the doctrine and organization to support an assisting, integrating, and intervening capability.

Moreover, the two doctrinal works that most directly affect the theory and practice of low-intensity conflict (Air Force Manual 2–5, *Tactical Air Operations—Special Air Warfare*, and Air Force Manual 3–5, *Special Air Warfare Tactics*) have not been revised recently. (The most recent version of AFM 2–5 was published on 10 March 1967 and has not been revised or amended since that date; AFM 3–5 was published on 18 March 1966, amended in 1968, and has been dormant since.) These two manuals should be the bible on what the Air Force should be doing if it is to participate in low-intensity conflicts. Yet, both manuals refer to organizational structures and air power capabilities that have not existed for many years. Some important weapon systems capabilities, such as the inflight refueling capability of the AC-130, MC-130, and HH-53, are not mentioned in these obsolete manuals. Further, AFM 2–5 describes the Special Air Warfare Center (SAWC) as the Air Force focal point for training, advice, guidance, and recommendations on special operations matters. Within the SAWC, it tasks the 1st Combat Applications Group to develop tactics, techniques, and equipment for the various air command wings. But as shown in the preceding chapter, the Special Air Warfare Center and its highly capable specialized units have long since faded from the Air Force.
from the Air Force.

AFM 2–5 lists a wide range of responsibilities for the special operations force, including search and rescue, military civic action, country team surveys and planning, mobile training teams, close air support, interdiction, and tactical air reconnaissance. Those tasks, reflecting a capability that existed in the 1960s could be easily adapted to our proposed philosophy of assisting, integrating, and intervening; but the capability is gone. Furthermore, AFM 3–5 provides detailed tactical guidance for aircraft no longer available for the special operations missions.

The point is that rethinking special operations doctrine *in new terms* must begin now. But before the doctrine can be written, the Air Force must decide at what level it wishes to participate in low-intensity conflicts. At present the Air Force special operations force can participate only in a very narrow part of the low-intensity conflict spectrum. It can effectively insert and extract small-sized forces covertly, and it can carry out one-time raids, but the ability of Air Force special operations forces to participate for longer time periods has waned considerably. If the Air Force wishes only to provide airlift for special operations and a highly specialized infiltration or "exfiltration" capability, current organizational structures are adequate. However, if we as an institution accept the notion that low-intensity conflict involves a broad scope of activity requiring a wide range of military options, then thought must be given to a special operations force of greatly expanded capability.

A Special Air Warfare Center for Today's World

The Special Air Warfare Center, as originally conceived, provides a model for us to work toward. The center worked to build US Air Force capability to assist, integrate with local forces, and intervene in small wars. I propose reestablishing and reinvigorating the Special Air Warfare Center. The chart at figure 14 shows the major functional entities that would be essential to a new special air warfare center or any other such Air Force organization that was designed to participate at all levels of activity in the low-intensity conflict spectrum. The mission of such an organization would be, as suggested previously, to provide military options for United States decision makers considering involvement in low-intensity conflicts. These options would include programs to assist or integrate with third world air forces or to intervene directly in a conflict if necessary. This organization would maximize Air Force participation in small wars. Although a highly idealized vision, this model provides the basis for discussion within the Air Force about what the proper role for a revitalized center in low-intensity conflicts should be.

This infrastructure is what will make the operational units—the aircraft and the people—effective in the missions they are to achieve. In a low-intensity warfare unit, the rapport between the operators and the support organizations will have to be extraordinarily good. Thus, the infrastructure elements of the center should be collocated with the operational units if the special warfare wings are to be effective.

Liaison

Although a separate directorate to handle liaison functions (fig. 13, chap. 6) might seem incongruous in an air division, interagency, interservice, and intraservice liaison will be a key factor in the effectiveness of an Air Force unit dedicated to low-intensity conflict. Any kind of military activity in the third world will require extensive cooperation between many agencies. At a minimum an Air Force unit designed for low-intensity conflict would need to maintain a close working relationship with the US Army Special Operations Command at Fort Bragg, the Navy's sea-air-land (SEAL) teams, the Defense Department international security affairs office, the State Department, numerous Air Staff agencies including the Directorate of International Programs (HQ USAF/PRI) and the Plans Directorate (HQ USAF/XOX), the Defense Security Assistance Agency, the Office of Joint Chiefs of Staff, and major Air Force commands. Whether the mission is making a one-time raid as in Son Tay or Iran, providing technical assistance on a short- or long-term basis to a friendly country, or

PLAN FOR USAF PARTICIPATION IN LIC

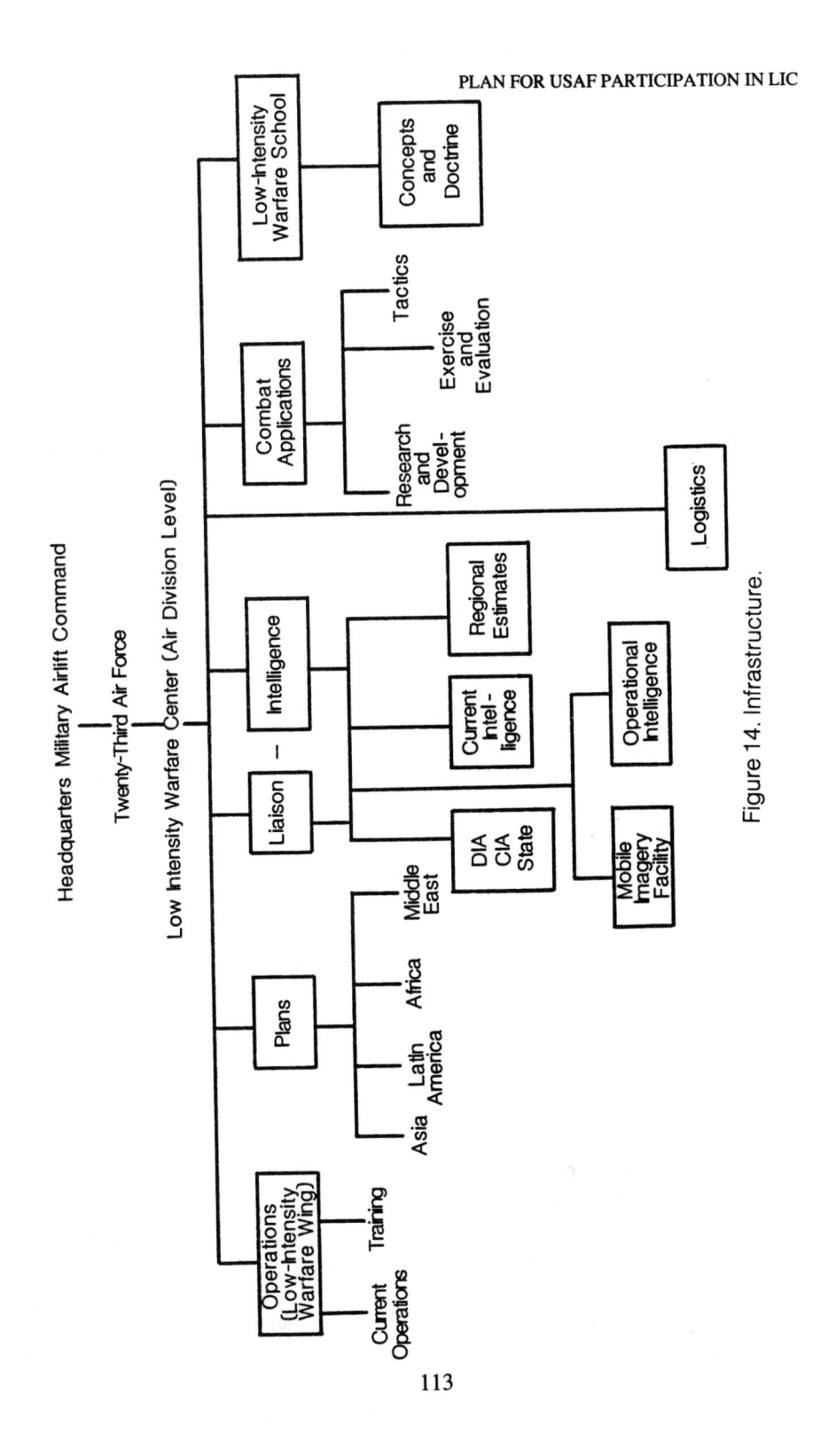

Figure 14. Infrastructure.

preparing to intervene with advisors or combat forces, the US Air Force unit will need to work with the policy-making elements of the US government and other US military services. A continuously operating liaison unit will be able to organize joint operations more easily, and can make an Air Force role in any interdisciplinary approach to resolving a low-intensity conflict more effective.

Operations and Training

The operations directorate would provide normal operations and training support for the center. The composition of this directorate, which would control the aircraft and aircrews of the center, will be discussed in detail under the topic of force structure.

Plans

The plans directorate would be the heart of any assistance provided by the Air Force in low-intensity conflict. It would be divided into regional branches (Asia, Latin America, Africa, and Middle East at a minimum) and would provide support for all Air Force assistance programs abroad. Thus, the plans directorate would provide a core of expertise to assist any Air Force mobile training teams sent on specific assistance missions, and could provide advice to decision makers in Washington on proposed aid packages for friends and allies.

The center's plans staff would maintain close contact with Air Staff regional planners and DOD international security affairs project officers. The center's plans directorate would gather and maintain information on conditions in all regions. The staff would be composed of trained area specialists with thorough language training; their knowledge of the political-military situations in the countries of each region would be unsurpassed. Because of their expertise, the people in this directorate would be an invaluable advisory resource to the hard-pressed action officers of the Air Staff, who often have to make decisions on military aid proposals with minimal background information. In addition, the center's plans people would be responsible for evaluating likely future problem spots in the areas for which they were responsible. That is, they would continuously evaluate US interests in each region and develop priorities for each. Then they would develop potential assistance, integration, or intervention scenarios against which the center would test its people, equipment, doctrine, and tactics.

Intelligence

While the plans directorate would build knowledge oriented to operations and scenarios, the intelligence directorate would build data bases on each region, keep track of current intelligence developments, and have the prime responsibility for developing political-military estimates on key countries. As suggested throughout this paper, knowledge about target areas is the key to participating successfully in low-intensity conflicts. Superb intelligence was the key factor that made British air control work. Knowing the people and the country where they were operating enabled the British forces to develop the doctrine and tactics that made their air control concept so successful. By comparison, US ignorance of the capabilities of the Royal Moroccan Air Force and the political-military realities in Morocco (and in the United States) caused our efforts to assist Morocco during the SA-6 crisis to fall short of the mark. Clearly the intelligence and planning functions would complement each other and would have to work together closely to achieve the greatest productivity.

The intelligence directorate would also have a strong capability to support immediate operational requirements, separate from its current estimative and basic intelligence functions. It would have to meet the intelligence requirements for one-time special operations missions; this effort would require extreme protective measures to ensure security of the operation. The intelligence staff would also have to develop the procedures to provide intelligence assistance to host countries in assistance, integration, and intervention scenarios. Permanently assigned liaison officers from DIA, CIA, and the State Department would be invaluable in developing, and eventually standardizing, procedures for transferring intelligence to friendly third world countries.

Another important intelligence function would be to tailor specific intelligence techniques and equipment to support the operational assets of the low-intensity conflict center. Should a conflict expand beyond the pure assistance stage to a level where Air Force units are tasked to assist a friendly air force or to intervene directly, our units would need this tailored intelligence. The intelligence directorate should include a fully mobile, miniature imagery-processing facility. This unit should be able to process photographic and radar imagery from aircraft and to receive finished intelligence from national sources. This facility would also serve as the core for a most important teaching asset. As exemplified in the Morocco-Polisario case study, many third world air forces need help in developing viable air intelligence collection, processing, interpretation, and dissemination capabilities. A mobile intelligence processing center could deploy to any third world country and could train third world air forces in intelligence techniques.

Combat Applications

The combat applications directorate would be a direct descendant of the 1st Combat Applications Group of the original Special Air Warfare Center. Working closely with the operational wing, the combat applications directorate would develop and test equipment for use in low-intensity conflict arenas. Its primary functions would be to provide training in individual combat skills, to train units to operate with host forces, and to train units to operate in conjunction with other US services. It would also maintain contact with the research and development community to keep abreast of technological developments that could be adapted to low-intensity conflicts.

In addition, the combat applications directorate would develop and evaluate exercises and document new tactics for use by the center's forces as well as by third world countries. A realistic and creative program of exercises is a useful way of expanding one's knowledge about the capabilities and limitations of sister services, the services of potential allies and friends, and one's own unit. During the course of an exercise, new or innovative tactics can be developed. Regardless of the exercise, special attention must be given to developing realistic scenarios. The combat applications directorate could draw on expertise from the plans and intelligence directorates in developing these training scenarios. Exercises must be held often and with as many "real" players as possible. Operating with the forces of the US Army and Navy would contribute to effective joint operations when those are necessary; operating with the air forces of friendly or allied nations would yield valuable insight into the real and potential capabilities of those forces. It could also provide invaluable experience in operating in future potential battlefields.

Logistics

The logistics directorate, as in any Air Force organization, would have the essential task of making sure proper supplies are available for the mission. A normal Air Force logistics unit would be acceptable for this new organization, with a few exceptions. It needs to have a priority, no-wait procurement capability for specialized items that may be required for the low-intensity conflict mission. One-time raids, an important part of that mission, may require a few pieces of specialized equipment that need to be procured under conditions of strict secrecy for security purposes. Such extraordinary requirements generate unusual demands on any logistics system that need to be anticipated and allowed for. The logistics directorate needs to be able to fabricate and modify equipment to meet the special needs of the organization.

Low-Intensity Warfare School

The proposed low-intensity warfare school would operate much as the Special Operations School has over the past several years. However, it would put greater emphasis on teaching US personnel techniques to prepare them to train friendly third world air forces better. Intensive courses in cross-cultural relations, language training in coordination with the Defense Language Institute, and instruction in the courses currently being taught would become part of the school's mission. In addition, the school should have a separate concepts and doctrine section. As the center becomes involved in various levels of low-intensity conflict, a tremendous influx of knowledge and experience will begin to accumulate at the center. The school should have the additional responsibility of gleaning what is important from that experience, preserving it, and, where appropriate, including it in the constantly evolving doctrinal process. The school would quickly become the Air Force focal point for new thinking regarding low-intensity conflict.

Force Structure

Structuring forces to be assigned to the suggested low-intensity conflict center will be critical to any potential for success by the Air Force in future small wars. Deciding on the quantity and types of aircraft to be operated by this center will be a difficult matter. At this point quantitative issues are less important than the qualitative requirements for such a unit. Figure 15 shows the basic aircraft of a low-intensity conflict wing.

The capabilities provided by the C-130s and helicopters currently assigned to the Air Force special operations force have been discussed previously. As noted, they provide a superb infiltration and extraction capability, a modest firepower delivery and reconnaissance capability, and a minimal psychological warfare capability. These aircraft are best suited for one-time raids. However, if the philosophy of assisting, integrating, or intervening that is espoused here is adopted, the low-intensity conflict center will need additional types of assets.

The major assets currently assigned to special operations—C-130s and heavy helicopters—are extraordinarily complex and, therefore, difficult to maintain: they are ill-suited for the assistance mission. Moreover, few third world countries can maintain the complex electronics of these systems, much less afford to buy them; they also have little need for these aircraft. Their needs are more traditional than unconventional. They need reconnaissance, transport, and strike aircraft adapted to their specialized environments.

Two of the needs of a typical third world air force correspond to weak spots in the current US Air Force special operations force—reconnaissance and strike. Our Air Force special operations force has a limited reconnaissance capability in its C-130s, and a very specialized strike capability in its AC-130s. The low-intensity conflict center should have a squadron of Northrup F-20 Tigersharks since this aircraft is being pushed as the future fighter for many third world countries. Developing the tactics and techniques for using this aircraft in a variety of roles will determine if it will be a useful addition to third world air

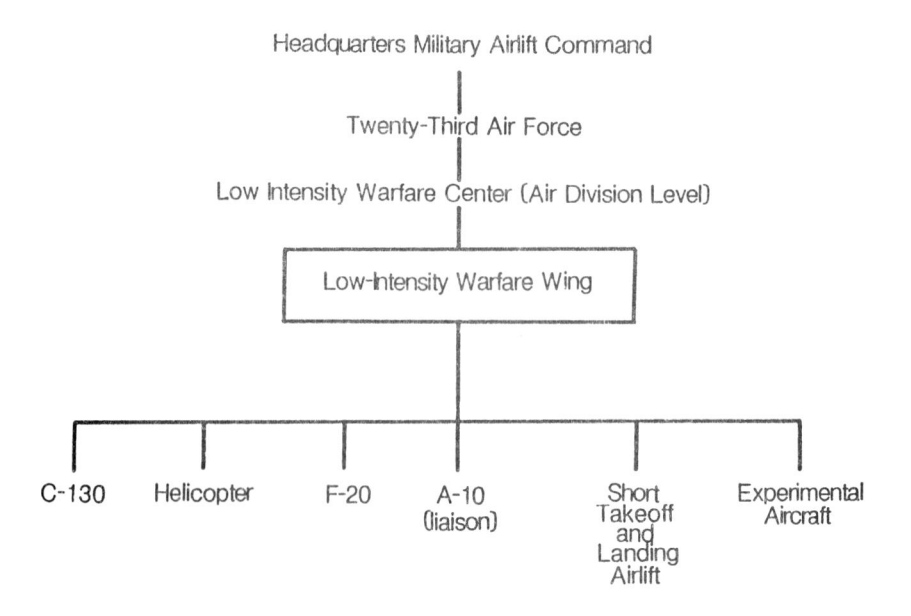

```
                Headquarters Military Airlift Command
                                 |
                      Twenty-Third Air Force
                                 |
            Low Intensity Warfare Center (Air Division Level)
                                 |
                   ┌─────────────────────────────┐
                   │   Low-Intensity Warfare Wing │
                   └─────────────────────────────┘
                                 |
   ┌─────────┬──────────┬────────┼────────┬─────────────┬──────────────┐
 C-130   Helicopter    F-20     A-10      Short         Experimental
                               (liaison)  Takeoff       Aircraft
                                          and
                                          Landing
                                          Airlift
```

Figure 15. Operations.

forces. Theoretically the F-20 could be adapted to reconnaissance, strike (deep and close), and air defense roles. Because of this flexibility and the designed-in simplicity of the aircraft, it should be a welcome addition to most third world air forces. But third world countries often are reluctant to buy what they consider to be second-string fighters of the superpowers. Normally, a third world country will want a top-of-the-line fighter such as the F-15 or F-16, regardless of the reality of the threat faced and the exorbitant initial and follow-on costs of the super-sophisticated front-line fighters. It is very hard to convince commanders of a third world air force that they should buy an F-5 and F-20 when they see that the US Air Force has neither aircraft in its combat inventory. An F-20 unit as part of the US Air Force low-intensity conflict center would perhaps make selling the F-20 abroad a good deal easier.

More important than the commercial aspects of an Air Force F-20 unit is the potential value of such as unit to developing a low-intensity conflict strategy for the US Air Force. With such a unit, the US Air Force could devise and test tactics for using a moderately sophisticated aircraft in small wars. It would also be the ideal aircraft around which to build the assistance, integration, and intervention concept. As the Air Force developed tactics for using the F-20, those tactics could be passed on to friendly third world air forces. Training exercises between the US Air Force and host country air forces would refine those techniques and provide the groundwork should the Air Force need a unit to integrate with a host nation air force. This unit would be ideal for serving as a third world Red Flag team; it could fly with and teach specialized tactics to host nations' units—a capability sorely lacking in the US Air Force, as we saw in the Morocco SA-6 crisis. And, an Air Force F-20 unit could be supported more easily than F-15 or F-16 units in a beleaguered third world country. Using the specifically trained and experienced people of a low-intensity conflict center, the US Air Force could respond as effectively in many parts of the world as do the French in Africa (assuming we develop the political will and finesse to operate like the French). A modest amount of easily supported US air power could play an important role in many third world conflicts.

The low-intensity conflict center should have access to other strike resources as well. Perhaps a general purpose A-10 unit could be designated to train with the center to develop tactics appropriate to low-intensity conflicts. The A-37 (fig. 16), a workhorse in Vietnam, might also be resurrected by the center. That aircraft is currently being operated by several third world countries and could have a role similar to that proposed for the F-20 within the center.

Airlift within the current special operations force is being handled by the modest C-130 and helicopter assets assigned to the command. The short takeoff and landing (STOL) aircraft that were so much a part of the special operations force of the 1960s have been largely purged from the Air Force. The C-7A Caribous (fig. 17) and C-123 Providers (fig. 18) are no longer in the active inventory; the former are about to be phased out from the reserves and only a few of the latter are operated by the Air National Guard. Reactivated C-7s and C-123s could provide a valuable and cheap intratheater capability. When combined with helicopters, a modest STOL fixed-wing force could be a valuable asset in low-intensity conflict scenarios. OV-10s (fig. 19) might be used for a reconnaissance role.

Of course, developing appropriate follow-on aircraft specifically designed for those kinds of conflicts would be a primary goal of both the operational flying units and the combat applications directorate. The US aircraft industry has never had reason to exert its energies toward developing an aircraft for low-intensity conflict. The Air Force has never generated the doctrine or the operational requirement to develop such an aircraft. The proposed low-intensity conflict center would be the ideal organization to develop the expertise leading to a viable proposal for a new aircraft specifically designed for low-intensity conflict. The options are enormous: vertical-takeoff aircraft, superlight aircraft, multipurpose fighters, tilt-rotor aircraft—all are possibilities.

Looking Ahead

This paper has suggested that small wars will be with us for the foreseeable future and that our ability to cope with large-scale conventional conflict does not

THE AIR FORCE ROLE IN LOW-INTENSITY CONFLICT

Figure 16. A-37 Low-Level Attack Fighter.

PLAN FOR USAF PARTICIPATION IN LIC

Figure 17. C-7A Caribou Short Takeoff and Landing Transport.

Figure 18. C-123 Provider Attack Transport.

Figure 19. OV-10 Light-Armed Reconnaissance and Attack Aircraft.

necessarily mean that we can cope with small wars. The least likely kinds of conflict—strategic nuclear exchange, large-scale conventional war in Europe, and a major Rapid Deployment Force movement to the Persian Gulf—currently drive resource allocation as well as strategic and doctrinal thinking. While this is true of all the services to some degree, the Air Force seems especially negligent in defining its role and developing a doctrine applicable to small wars, or as we have called it here, low-intensity conflict.

The chart at figure 20 summarizes how a newly revitalized and renamed USAF Special Air Warfare Center would provide the basis for effective US Air Force participation in current and future small wars. Running vertically along the left-hand margin of the chart is a hierarchy for looking at any war. Vision, strategy, operations, and tactics are the vital elements that make up a war. Vision is the policy-level concept of what a nation or institution hopes to achieve in a conflict situation. In the case of low-intensity conflicts, the US vision can be stated bluntly: to exert control or influence in support of US policy in the third world. Boldly stated, this sounds chauvinistic and unrealistic. Perhaps so. For the United States to develop an overall small-war capability, US political resolve must become firm and the American people must support our need to act abroad. The problems associated with attaining a vision for active US involvement in the third world are vast. Here I am dealing only with establishing one small capability in the overall resources—political, military, and economic—that must be dedicated to the problem of low-intensity conflict.

Below national vision, national strategies or plans are developed to implement that vision. Operations are programs within the overall plan, and tactics are specific activities within operations. The experience that would flow from the proposed low-intensity conflict center would be the basis for developing air tactics for use in various low-intensity warfare situations. The conceptual framework expressed by the ideas of assisting, integrating, and intervening in small wars provides the philosophic basis for developing an Air Force capability to participate in small wars. Finally, figure 15 shows that the proposed US Air Force low-intensity warfare center would be in close coordination with the rather diverse collection of agencies that are now concerned with low-intensity conflicts.

An organization based on the USAF Special Air Warfare Center of the 1960s should be the focal point for concentrating the Air Force people and equipment concerned with low-intensity conflict. Before such a unit could be established, however, the Air Force must make an organizational commitment to developing ways of participating in low-intensity conflicts. From this commitment should come theoretical doctrine on applying air power in low-intensity conflict. As the new low-intensity conflict center takes shape, this theoretical doctrine would be tested and refined, eventually to become "true" doctrine. This process will be long, difficult, and unpopular but necessary if the Air Force is to have a meaningful role in the most likely kinds of future conflicts. As a result of the recent transfer of special operations assets from the Tactical Air Command to the

PLAN FOR USAF PARTICIPATION IN LIC

VISION → **EXERT CONTROL AND INFLUENCE IN SUPPORT OF U.S. POLICY IN THIRD WORLD**

STRATEGY
- ASSIST → AIR FORCE-TO-AIR FORCE / INTERDISCIPLINARY OPERATIONS / JOINT MILITARY OPERATIONS
- INTEGRATE → AIR FORCE-TO-AIR FORCE / INTERDISCIPLINARY OPERATIONS / JOINT MILITARY OPERATIONS

OPERATIONS
- INTERVENE → AIR POWER/JOINT SERVICE

TACTICS

{ COOPERATIVE FUNCTIONS WITH FRIENDLY FOREIGN FORCES, ESP TRANSITIONAL NATIONS.

UNILATERAL, OR WITH "FIRST WORLD" ALLIES. (FRANCE, GREAT BRITAIN, GERMANY) }

USAFE LOW-INTENSITY WARFARE CENTER
... DOCTRINE ...
... EXPERTISE ...

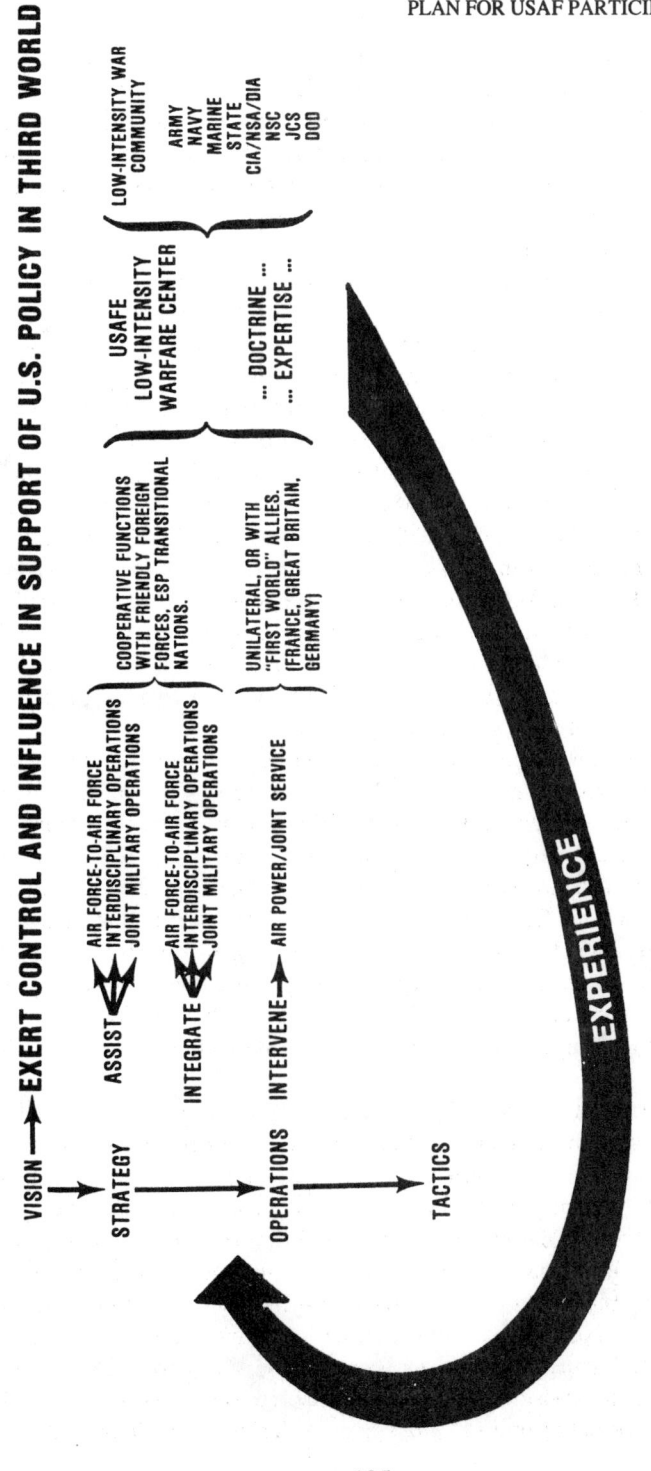

LOW-INTENSITY WAR COMMUNITY
ARMY
NAVY
MARINE
STATE
CIA/NSA/DIA
NSC
JCS
DOD

EXPERIENCE

Figure 20. Hierarchy of War Fighting.

Military Airlift Command, the US Air Force is in an ideal position to learn from the past and prepare forces capable of acting in a violent and uncertain, if not cataclysmic, world.

NOTES

CHAPTER 7

1. See Sam C. Sarkesian and William L. Scully, eds., *US Policy and Low-Intensity Conflict* (New York: National Defense Information Center, 1981), 11, and Robert B. Asprey, *War In the Shadows* (New York: Doubleday and Company, Inc., 1975), 159.
2. AFM 1-1, *Basic Aeospace Doctrine of the United States Air Force,* Department of the Air Force, 16 March 1984, 3-4.
3. Ibid.
4. Robert L. Brenchi, "USAF Special Operations: The Forgotten Force," Air War College Research Report No. AV-AWC-93-026 (Maxwell AFB, Ala., February 1983).
5. TACM 2-1, *Tactical Air Operations,* Headquarters Tactical Air Command, 15 April 1978, 4-57 to 4-58.
6. Draft AFM 1-1, dated 9 January 1983.
7. TACM 2-1, 5-54.
8. Department of the Air Force, *Air Force 2000* (11 June 1982), 93. (SECRET)
9. "USAF Beefing Up Low-Level Warfare Capabilities," *Tech Trends,* 3 March 1986, 3.

☆U.S. GOVERNMENT PRINTING OFFICE: 2001-636-471/40017